A New Philosophy:
Henri Bergson

Edouard Le Roy

COSIMO CLASSICS
NEW YORK

A New Philosophy: Henri Bergson
© 2005 Cosimo, Inc.
All rights reserved. No part of this book may be used or reproduced in any manner whatsoever without prior written permission except in the case of brief quotations embodied in critical articles or reviews.
For information, address:

Cosimo, P.O. Box 416
Old Chelsea Station
New York, NY 10113-0416

or visit our website at:
www.cosimobooks.com

A New Philosophy: Henri Bergson originally published by Henry Holt & Co. in 1913.

Library of Congress Cataloging-in-Publication Data
A catalog record for this book is available from the Library of Congress

Cover design by www.wiselephant.com

ISBN: 1-59605-332-1

A NEW PHILOSOPHY
HENRI BERGSON

PREFACE

THIS little book is due to two articles published under the same title in the *Revue des Deux Mondes*, 1st and 15th February 1912.

Their object was to present Mr Bergson's philosophy to the public at large, giving as short a sketch as possible, and describing, without too minute details, the general trend of his movement. These articles I have here reprinted intact. But I have added, in the form of continuous notes, some additional explanations on points which did not come within the scope of investigation in the original sketch.

I need hardly add that my work, though thus far complete, does not in any way claim to be a profound critical study. Indeed, such a study, dealing with a thinker who has not yet said his last word, would to-day be premature. I have simply aimed at writing an introduction which will make it easier to read and understand

Mr Bergson's works, and serve as a preliminary guide to those who desire initiation in the new philosophy.

I have therefore firmly waived all the paraphernalia of technical discussions, and have made no comparisons, learned or otherwise, between Mr Bergson's teaching and that of older philosophies.

I can conceive no better method of misunderstanding the point at issue, I mean the simple unity of productive intuition, than that of pigeon-holing names of systems, collecting instances of resemblance, making up analogies, and specifying ingredients. An original philosophy is not meant to be studied as a mosaic which takes to pieces, a compound which analyses, or a body which dissects. On the contrary, it is by considering it as a living act, not as a rather clever discourse, by examining the peculiar excellence of its soul rather than the formation of its body, that the inquirer will succeed in understanding it. Properly speaking, I have only applied to Mr Bergson the method which he himself justifiably prescribes in a recent article (*Revue de Métaphysique et de Morale*, November 1911), the only method, in fact, which is in all senses of the word fully "exact." I shall none the less be glad if these brief pages can be of any interest to professional philosophers, and have endeavoured, as far as possible, to allow them to trace, under the concise formulæ employed, the scheme which I have refused to develop.

It has become evident to me that even to-day the interpretation of Mr Bergson's position is in many cases full of faults, which it would undoubtedly be worth while to assist in removing. I may or may not have succeeded in my attempt, but such, at any rate, is the precise end I had in view.

In conclusion, I may say that I have not had the honour of being Mr Bergson's pupil; and, at the time when I became acquainted with his outlook, my own direct reflection on science and life had already produced in me similar trains of thought. I found in his work the striking realisation of a presentiment and a desire. This "correspondence," which I have not exaggerated, proved at once a help and a hindrance to me in entering into the exact comprehension of so profoundly original a doctrine. The reader will thus understand that I think it in place to quote my authority to him in the following lines which Mr Bergson kindly wrote me after the publication of the articles reproduced in this volume:

"Underneath and beyond the method you have caught the *intention* and the *spirit*. . . . Your study could not be more conscientious or true to the original. As it advances, condensation increases in a marked degree: the reader becomes aware that the explanation is undergoing a progressive involution similar to the involution by which we determine *the reality of Time*. To produce this feeling, much more has been necessary than a close study of my works: it has required deep sympathy of thought, the power, in fact, of rethinking the subject in a personal and original manner. Nowhere is this sympathy more in evidence than in your concluding pages, where in a few words you point out the possibilities of further developments of the doctrine. In this direction I should myself say exactly what you have said."

PARIS, 28*th March* 1912.

CONTENTS

PREFACE v

GENERAL VIEW

I. METHOD 1
Scope of Henri Bergson's Philosophy. Material and Authorities. Investigation of Common-sense. Value of Science. Perception Discussed. Practical Life and Reality. Concepts and Symbolism. Intuition and Analysis. Use of Metaphor. The Philosopher's Task.

II. TEACHING 60
The Ego. Space and Number. Parallelism. Henri Bergson's View of Mind and Matter. Qualitative Continuity. Memory. Real Duration Heterogeneous. Liberty and Determinism. Meaning of Reality. Evolution and Automatism. Triumph of Man. The Vital Impulse. Objections Refuted. Place of Religion in the New Philosophy.

ADDITIONAL EXPLANATIONS

I. HENRI BERGSON'S WORK AND THE GENERAL DIRECTIONS OF CONTEMPORARY THOUGHT . 126
Mathematics and Philosophy. The Inert and the Living. Realism and Positivism. Henri Bergson and the Intuition of Duration.

	PAGE
II. IMMEDIACY	142

Necessity of Criticism. Utilitarianism of Common-sense. Perception of Immediacy.

III. THEORY OF PERCEPTION 156

Pure and Ordinary Perception. Kant's Position. Relation of Perception to Matter. Complete Experience.

IV. CRITIQUE OF LANGUAGE 167

Dynamic Schemes. Dangers of Language. The Eleatic Dialectic. Scientific Thought and the Task of Intuition. Discussion of Change.

V. THE PROBLEM OF CONSCIOUSNESS: DURATION AND LIBERTY 185

States as Phases in Duration. The Scientific View of Time. Duration and Freedom. Liberty and Determinism in the Light of Henri Bergson's Philosophy.

VI. THE PROBLEM OF EVOLUTION: LIFE AND MATTER 201

Evolution and Creation. Laws of Conservation and Degradation. Quantity and Quality. Secondary Value of Matter.

VII. THE PROBLEM OF KNOWLEDGE: ANALYSIS AND INTUITION 210

Difficulties of Kant's Position. Insufficiency of Intelligence. Henri Bergson and the Problem of Reason. Geometric and Vital Types of Order.

VIII. CONCLUSION 223

Moral and Religious Problems. Henri Bergson's Position.

A NEW PHILOSOPHY

GENERAL VIEW

I
METHOD

THERE is a thinker whose name is to-day on everybody's lips, who is deemed by acknowledged philosophers worthy of comparison with the greatest, and who, with his pen as well as his brain, has overleapt all technical obstacles, and won himself a reading both outside and inside the schools. Beyond any doubt, and by common consent, Mr Henri Bergson's work will appear to future eyes among the most characteristic, fertile, and glorious of our era. It marks a never-to-be-forgotten date in history; it opens up a phase of metaphysical thought; it lays down a principle of development the limits of which are indeterminable; and it is after cool consideration, with full consciousness of the exact value of words, that we are able to pronounce the revolution which it effects equal in importance to that effected by Kant, or even by Socrates.

Everybody, indeed, has become aware of this more or less clearly. Else how are we to explain, except through such recognition, the sudden striking spread of this new philosophy which, by its learned rigorism, precluded the likelihood of so rapid a triumph?

Twenty years have sufficed to make its results felt far beyond traditional limits: and now its influence is alive and working from one pole of thought to the other; and the active leaven contained in it can be seen already extending to the most varied and distant spheres: in social and political spheres, where from opposite points, and not without certain abuses, an attempt is already being made to wrench it in contrary directions; in the sphere of religious speculation, where it has been more legitimately summoned to a distinguished, illuminative, and beneficent career; in the sphere of pure science, where, despite old separatist prejudices, the ideas sown are pushing up here and there; and lastly, in the sphere of art, where there are indications that it is likely to help certain presentiments, which have till now remained obscure, to become conscious of themselves. The moment is favourable to a study of Mr Bergson's philosophy; but in the face of so many attempted methods of employment, some of them a trifle premature, the point of paramount importance, applying Mr Bergson's own method to himself, is to study his philosophy in itself, for itself, in its profound trend and its authenticated action, without claiming to enlist it in the ranks of any cause whatsoever.

I

Mr Bergson's readers will undergo at almost every page they read an intense and singular experience. The curtain drawn between ourselves and reality, enveloping everything including ourselves in its illusive folds, seems of a sudden to fall, dissipated by enchantment, and display to the mind depths of light till then undreamt, in which reality itself, contemplated face to face for the first time, stands fully revealed. The revelation is overpowering, and once vouchsafed will never afterwards be forgotten.

Nothing can convey to the reader the effects of this direct and intimate mental vision. Everything which he thought he knew already finds new birth and vigour in the clear light of morning: on all hands, in the glow of dawn, new intuitions spring up and open out; we feel them big with infinite consequences, heavy and saturated with life. Each of them is no sooner blown than it appears fertile for ever. And yet there is nothing paradoxical or disturbing in the novelty. It is a reply to our expectation, an answer to some dim hope. So vivid is the impression of truth, that afterwards we are even ready to believe we recognise the revelation as if we had always darkly anticipated it in some mysterious twilight at the back of consciousness.

Afterwards, no doubt, in certain cases, incertitude reappears, sometimes even decided objections. The reader, who at first was under a magic spell, corrects his thought, or at least hesitates. What he has seen is still at bottom so new, so unexpected, so far removed from familiar conceptions. For this surging wave of thought our mind contains none of those ready-cut channels which render comprehension easy. But whether, in the long run, we each of us give or refuse complete or partial adhesion, all of us, at least, have received a regenerating shock, an internal upheaval not readily silenced: the network of our intellectual habits is broken ; henceforth a new leaven works and ferments in us ; we shall no longer think as we used to think ; and be we pupils or critics, we cannot mistake the fact that we have here a principle of integral renewal for ancient philosophy and its old and timeworn problems.

It is obviously impossible to sketch in brief all the aspects and all the wealth of so original a work. Still less shall I be able to answer here the many questions which arise. I must decide to pass rapidly over the technical detail of clear, closely-argued, and penetrating discussions ; over the scope and exactness of the evidence borrowed from the most diverse positive sciences ; over the marvellous dexterity of the psychological analysis ; over the magic of a style which can call up what words cannot express. The solidity of the construction will not be evidenced in these pages, nor its austere and subtle beauty. But what I do at all costs wish to bring out, in shorter form, in this new philosophy, is its directing idea and general movement.

In such an undertaking, where the end is to understand rather than to judge, criticism ought to take second place. It is more profitable to attempt to feel oneself into the heart of the teaching, to relive its genesis, to perceive the principle of organic unity, to come at the mainspring. Let our reading be a course of meditation which we live. The only true homage we can render to the masters of thought consists in ourselves thinking, as far as we can do so, in their train, under their inspiration, and along the paths which they have opened up.

In the case before us this road is landmarked by several books which it will be sufficient to study one after the other, and take successively as the text of our reflections.

In 1889 Mr Bergson made his appearance with an *Essay on the Immediate Data of Consciousness.*

This was his doctor's thesis. Taking up his position inside the human personality, in its inmost mind, he endeavoured to lay hold of the depths of life and free action in their commonly overlooked and fugitive originality.

Some years later, in 1896, passing this time to the externals of consciousness, the contact surface between things and the ego, he published *Matter and Memory*, a masterly study of perception and recollection, which he himself put forward as an inquiry into the relation between body and mind. In 1907 he followed with *Creative Evolution*, in which the new metaphysic was outlined in its full breadth, and developed with a wealth of suggestion and perspective opening upon the distances of infinity; universal evolution, the meaning of life, the nature of mind and matter, of intelligence and instinct, were the great problems here treated, ending in a general critique of knowledge and a completely original definition of philosophy.

These will be our guides which we shall carefully follow, step by step. It is not, I must confess, without some apprehension that I undertake the task of summing up so much research, and of condensing into a few pages so many and such new conclusions.

Mr Bergson excels, even on points of least significance, in producing the feeling of unfathomed depths and infinite levels. Never has anyone better understood how to fulfil the philosopher's first task, in pointing out the hidden mystery in everything. With him we see all at once the concrete thickness and inexhaustible extension of the most familiar reality, which has always been before our eyes, where before we were aware only of the external film.

Do not imagine that this is simply a poetical

delusion. We must be grateful if the philosopher uses exquisite language and writes in a style which abounds in living images. These are rare qualities. But let us avoid being duped by a show of printed matter: these unannotated pages are supported by positive science submitted to the most minute inspection. One day, in 1901, at the French Philosophical Society, Mr Bergson related the genesis of *Matter and Memory*.

"Twelve years or so before its appearance, I had set myself the following problem: 'What would be the teaching of the physiology and pathology of to-day upon the ancient question of the connection between physical and moral to an unprejudiced mind, determined to forget all speculation in which it has indulged on this point, determined also to neglect, in the enunciations of philosophers, all that is not pure and simple statement of fact?' I set myself to solve the problem, and I very soon perceived that the question was susceptible of a provisional solution, and even of precise formulation, only if restricted to the problem of memory. In memory itself I was forced to determine bounds which I had afterwards to narrow considerably. After confining myself to the recollection of words

I saw that the problem, as stated, was still too broad, and that, to put the question in its most precise and interesting form, I should have to substitute the recollection of the sound of words. The literature on aphasia is enormous. I took five years to sift it. And I arrived at this conclusion, that between the psychological fact and its corresponding basis in the brain there must be a relation which answers to none of the ready-made concepts furnished us by philosophy."

Certain characteristics of Mr Bergson's manner will be remarked throughout: his provisional effort of forgetfulness to recreate a new and untrammelled mind; his mixture of positive inquiry and bold invention; his stupendous reading; his vast pioneer work carried on with indefatigable patience; his constant correction by criticism, informed of the minutest details and swift to follow up each of them at every turn. With a problem which would at first have seemed secondary and incomplete, but which reappears as the subject deepens and is thereby metamorphosed, he connects his entire philosophy; and so well does he blend the whole and breathe upon it the breath of life that the final statement leaves the reader with an impression of sovereign ease.

Examples will be necessary to enable us, even to a feeble extent, to understand this proceeding better. But before we come to examples, a preliminary question requires examination. In the preface to his first *Essay* Mr Bergson defined the principle of a method which was afterwards to reappear in its identity throughout his various works; and we must recall the terms he employed.

"We are forced to express ourselves in words, and we think, most often, in space. To put it another way, language compels us to establish between our ideas the same clear and precise distinctions, and the same break in continuity, as between material objects. This assimilation is useful in practical life and necessary in most sciences. But we are right in asking whether the insuperable difficulties of certain philosophical problems do not arise from the fact that we persist in placing non-spatial phenomena next one another in space, and whether, if we did away with the vulgar illustrations round which we dispute, we should not sometimes put an end to the dispute."

That is to say, it is stated to be the

philosopher's duty from the outset to renounce the usual forms of analytic and synthetic thought, and to achieve a direct intuitional effort which shall put him in immediate contact with reality. Without doubt it is this question of method which demands our first attention. It is the leading question. Mr Bergson himself presents his works as "essays" which do not aim at "solving the greatest problems all at once," but seek merely "to define the method and disclose the possibility of applying it on some essential points."[1] It is also a delicate question, for it dominates all the rest, and decides whether we shall fully understand what is to follow.

We must therefore pause here a moment. To direct us in this preliminary study we have an admirable *Introduction to Metaphysics*, which appeared as an article in the *Metaphysical and Moral Review* (January 1903): a short but marvellously suggestive *mémoire*, constituting the best preface to the reading of the books themselves. We may say in passing, that we should be grateful to Mr Bergson if he would have it bound in volume form, along with some other articles which are scarcely to be had at all to-day.

[1] Preface to *Creative Evolution*.

II

Every philosophy, prior to taking shape in a group of co-ordinated theses, presents itself, in its initial stage, as an attitude, a frame of mind, a method. Nothing can be more important than to study this starting-point, this elementary act of direction and movement, if we wish afterwards to arrive at the precise shade of meaning of the subsequent teaching. Here is really the fountain-head of thought; it is here that the form of the future system is determined, and here that contact with reality takes effect.

The last point, particularly, is vital. To return to the direct view of things beyond all figurative symbols, to descend into the inmost depths of being, to watch the throbbing life in its pure state, and listen to the secret rhythm of its inmost breath, to measure it, at least so far as measurement is possible, has always been the philosopher's ambition; and the new philosophy has not departed from this ideal. But in what light does it regard its task? That is the first point to clear up. For the problem is complex, and the goal distant.

"We are made as much, and more, for action than for thought," says Mr Bergson;

METHOD 13

"or rather, when we follow our natural impulse, it is to act that we think."[1] And again, "What we ordinarily call a *fact* is not reality such as it would appear to an immediate intuition, but an adaptation of reality to practical interests and the demands of social life."[2] Hence the question which takes precedence of all others is: *to distinguish in our common representation of the world, the fact in its true sense from the combinations which we have introduced in view of action and language.*

Now, to rediscover nature in her fresh springs of reality, it is not sufficient to abandon the images and conceptions invented by human initiative; still less is it sufficient to fling ourselves into the torrent of brute sensations. By so doing we are in danger of dissolving our thought in dream or quenching it in night.

Above all, we are in danger of committal to a path which it is impossible to follow. The philosopher is not free to begin the work of knowledge again upon other planes, with a mind which would be adequate to the new and virgin issue of a simple writ of oblivion.

At the time when critical reflection begins, we have already been long engaged in action

[1] *L'Évolution Créatrice*, p. 321.
[2] *Matière et Mémoire*, p. 201.

and science; by the training of individual life, as by hereditary and racial experience, our faculties of perception and conception, our senses and our understanding, have contracted habits, which are by this time unconscious and instinctive; we are haunted by all kinds of ideas and principles, so familiar to-day that they even pass unobserved. But what is it all worth?

Does it, in its present state, help us to know the nature of a disinterested intuition?

Nothing but a methodical examination of consciousness can tell us that; and it will take more than a renunciation of explicit knowledge to recreate in us a new mind, capable of grasping the bare fact exactly as it is: what we require is perhaps a penetrating reform, a kind of conversion.

The rational and perceptive function we term our intelligence emerges from darkness through a slowly lifting dawn. During this twilight period it has lived, worked, acted, fashioned and *informed* itself. On the threshold of philosophical speculation it is full of more or less concealed beliefs, which are literally prejudices, and branded with a secret mark influencing its every movement. Here is an actual situation. Exemption from it is beyond anyone's province. Whether we will or no, we are from the beginning of our inquiry immersed in a doctrine which disguises nature to us, and already at bottom constitutes a complete metaphysic. This we term *common-sense*, and positive science is itself only an extension and refinement of it. What is the value of this work performed without clear consciousness or critical attention? Does it bring us into true relation with things, into relation with pure consciousness?

This is our first and inevitable doubt, which requires solution.

But it would be a quixotic proceeding first to make a void in our mind, and afterwards to admit into it, one by one, after investigation, such and such a concept, or such and such a principle. The illusion of the clean sweep and total reconstruction can never be too vigorously condemned.

Is it from the void that we set out to think? Do we think in void, and with nothing? Common ideas of necessity form the groundwork for the broidery of our advanced thought. Further, even if we succeeded in our impossible task, should we, in so doing, have corrected the causes of error which are to-day graven upon the very structure of our intelligence, such as our past life has made it? These errors would not cease to act imperceptibly upon the work of revision intended to apply the remedy.

It is from within, by an effort of immanent purgation, that the necessary reform must be brought about. And philosophy's first task is to institute critical reflection upon the obscure beginnings of thought, with a view to shedding light upon its spontaneous virgin condition, but without any vain claim to lift it out of the current in which it is actually plunged.

One conclusion is already plain: *the groundwork of common-sense is sure, but the form is suspicious.*

In common-sense is contained, at any rate virtually and in embryo, all that can ever be attained of reality, for reality is verification, not construction.

Everything has its starting-point in construction and verification. Thus philosophical research can only be a conscious and deliberate return to the facts of primal intuition. But common-sense, being prepossessed in a practical direction, has doubtless subjected these facts to a process of interested alteration, which is artificial in proportion to the labour bestowed. Such is Mr Bergson's fundamental hypothesis, and it is far-reaching. "Many metaphysical difficulties probably arise from our habit of confounding speculation and practice; or of pushing an idea in the direction of utility, when we think we fathom it in theory; or, lastly, of employing in thought the forms of action."[1]

The work of reform will consist therefore in freeing our intelligence from its utilitarian habits, by endeavouring at the outset to become clearly conscious of them.

Notice how far presumption is in favour of our hypothesis. Whether we regard organic life in the genesis and preservation of the individual, or in the evolution of species, we see its natural direction to be towards utility: but the effort of thought comes after the effort of life; it is not added from outside, it is the continuance and the flower of the former effort. Must we not expect from this that it will preserve its former habits? And what do we actually observe? The first gleam of human intelligence in prehistoric times is revealed to us by an industry; the cut flint of the primitive caves marks the first stage of the road which was one day to end in the most sublime philosophies. Again, every science has begun

[1] Preface to *Matter and Memory*. First edition.

by practical arts. Indeed, our science of to-day, however disinterested it may have become, remains none the less in close relation with the demands of our action; it permits us to *speak of* and to *handle* things rather than to *see* them in their intimate and profound nature. Analysis, when applied to our operations of knowledge, shows us that our understanding parcels out, arrests, and quantifies, whereas reality, as it appears to immediate intuition, is a moving series, a flux of blended qualities.

That is to say, our understanding *solidifies* all that it touches. Have we not here exactly the essential postulates of action and speech? To speak, as to act, we must have separable elements, *terms* and *objects* which remain inert while the operation goes on, maintaining between themselves the constant relations which find their most perfect and ideal presentment in mathematics.

Everything tends, then, to incline us towards the hypothesis in question. Let us regard it henceforward as expressing a fact.

The forms of knowledge elaborated by common-sense were not originally intended to allow us to see reality as it is.

Their task was rather, and remains so, to enable us to grasp its practical aspect. It is for that they are made, not for philosophical speculation.

Now these forms nevertheless have existed in us as inveterate habits, soon becoming unconscious, even when we have reached the point of desiring knowledge for its own sake.

But in this new stage they preserve the bias of their original utilitarian function, and carry this mark with them everywhere, leaving it upon the fresh tasks which we are fain to make them accomplish.

An inner reform is therefore imperative to-day, if we are to succeed in unearthing and sifting, in our perception of nature, under the veinstone of practical symbolism, the true intuitional content.

This attempt at return to the standpoint of pure contemplation and disinterested experience is a task very different from the task of science. It is one thing to regard more and more or less and less closely with the eyes made for us by utilitarian evolution: it is another to labour at remaking for ourselves eyes capable of seeing, in order to see, and not in order to live.

Philosophy understood in this manner—and we shall see more and more clearly as we go on that there is no other legitimate method of understanding it—demands from us an almost violent act of reform and conversion.

The mind must turn round upon itself, invert the habitual direction of its thought, climb the hill down which its instinct towards action has carried it, and go to seek experience at its source, "above the critical bend where it inclines towards our practical use and becomes, properly speaking, human experience."[1] In short, by a twin effort of criticism and expansion, it must pass outside common-sense and synthetic understanding to return to pure intuition.

Philosophy consists in reliving the immediate over again, and in interpreting our rational science and everyday perception by its light. That, at least, is the first stage. We shall find afterwards that that is not all.

Here is a genuinely new conception of philosophy. Here, for the first time, philosophy is made specifically distinct from science, yet remains no less positive.

What science really does is to preserve the general attitude of common-sense, with its apparatus of forms and principles.

It is true that science develops and perfects it, refines and extends it, and even now and

[1] *Matter and Memory*, p. 203.

again corrects it. But science does not change either the direction or the essential steps.

In this philosophy, on the contrary, what is at first suspected and finally modified, is the setting of the points before the journey begins.

Not that, in saying so, we mean to condemn science; but we must recognise its just limits. The methods of science proper are in their place and appropriate, and lead to a knowledge which is true (though still symbolical), so long as the object studied is the world of practical action, or, to put it briefly, the world of inert matter.

But soul, life, and activity escape it, and yet these are the spring and ultimate basis of everything: and it is the appreciation of this fact, with what it entails, that is new. And yet, new as Mr Bergson's conception of philosophy may deservedly appear, it does not any the less, from another point of view, deserve to be styled classic and traditional.

What it really defines is not so much a particular philosophy as philosophy itself, in its original function.

Everywhere in history we find its secret current at its task.

All great philosophers have had glimpses of it, and employed it in moments of discovery.

Only as a general rule they have not clearly recognised what they were doing, and so have soon turned aside.

But on this point I cannot insist without going into lengthy detail, and am obliged to refer the reader to the fourth chapter of *Creative Evolution*, where he will find the whole question dealt with.

One remark, however, has still to be made. Philosophy, according to Mr Bergson's conception, implies and demands time; it does not aim at completion all at once, for the mental reform in question is of the kind which requires gradual fulfilment. The truth which it involves does not set out to be a non-temporal essence, which a sufficiently powerful genius would be able, under pressure, to perceive in its entirety at one view; and that again seems to be very new.

I do not, of course, wish to abuse systems of philosophy. Each of them is an experience of thought, a moment in the life of thought, a method of exploring reality, a reagent which reveals an aspect. Truth undergoes analysis into systems as does light into colours.

But the mere name system calls up the static idea of a finished building. Here there is nothing of the kind. The new philosophy

METHOD

desires to be a proceeding as much as, and even more than, to be a system. It insists on being lived as well as thought. It demands that thought should work at living its true life, an inner life related to itself, effective, active, and creative, but not on that account directed towards external action. "And," says Mr Bergson, "it can only be constructed by the collective and progressive effort of many thinkers, and of many observers, completing, correcting, and righting one another."[1]

Let us see how it begins, and what is its generating act.

III

How are we to attain the immediate? How are we to realise this perception of pure fact which we stated to be the philosopher's first step?

Unless we can clear up this doubt, the end proposed will remain to our gaze an abstract and lifeless ideal. This is, then, the point which requires instant explanation. For there is a serious difficulty in which the very employment of the word "immediate" might lead us astray.

The *immediate*, in the sense which concerns

[1] Preface to *Creative Evolution*.

us, is not at all, or at least is no longer for us the *passive experience*, the indefinable something which we should inevitably receive, provided we opened our eyes and abstained from reflection.

As a matter of fact, we cannot abstain from reflection: reflection is to-day part of our very vision; it comes into play as soon as we open our eyes. So that, to come on the trail of the immediate, there must be effort and work. How are we to guide this effort? In what will this work consist? By what sign shall we be able to recognise that the result has been obtained?

These are the questions to be cleared up. Mr Bergson speaks of them chiefly in connection with the realities of consciousness, or, more generally speaking, of life. And it is here, in fact, that the consequences are most weighty and far-reaching. We shall need to refer to them again in detail. But to simplify my explanation, I will here choose another example: that of inert matter, of the perception on which the physical is based. It is in this case that the divergence between common perception and pure perception, however real it may be, assumes least proportions.

Therefore it appears most in place in the

sketch I desire to trace of an exceedingly complex work, where I can only hope, evidently, to indicate the main lines and general direction.

We readily believe that when we cast our eyes upon surrounding objects, we enter into them unresistingly and apprehend them all at once in their intrinsic nature. Perception would thus be nothing but simple passive registration. But nothing could be more untrue, if we are speaking of the perception which we employ without profound criticism in the course of our daily life. What we here take to be pure fact is, on the contrary, the last term in a highly complicated series of mental operations. And this term contains as much of us as of things.

In fact, all concrete perception comes up for analysis as an indissoluble mixture of *construction* and *fact*, in which the fact is only revealed through the construction, and takes on its complexion. We all know by experience how incapable the uneducated person is of explaining the simple appearance of the least fact, without embodying a crowd of false interpretations. We know to a less extent, but it is also true, that the most enlightened and adroit person proceeds in just the same manner: his interpretation is better, but it is still interpretation.

That is why accurate observation is so difficult; we see or we do not see, we notice such and such an aspect, we read this or that, according to our state of consciousness at the time, according to the direction of the investigation on which we are engaged.

Who was it defined art as *nature seen through a mind*? Perception, too, is an art.

This art has its processes, its conventions, and its tools. Go into a laboratory and study one of those complex instruments which make our senses finer or more powerful; each of them is literally a sheaf of materialised theories, and by means of it all acquired science is brought to bear on each new observation of the student. In exactly the same way our organs of sense are actual instruments constructed by the unconscious work of the mind in the course of biological evolution; they too sum up and give concrete form and expression to a system of enlightening theories. But that is not all. The most elementary psychology shows us the amount of thought, in the correct sense of the term, recollection, or inference, which enters into what we should be tempted to call pure perception.

Establishment of fact is not the simple reception of the faithful imprint of that fact; it is invariably interpreted, systematised, and placed in pre-existing forms which constitute veritable theoretical frames. That is why the child has to learn to perceive. There is an education of the senses which he acquires by long training. One day, with the aid of habit, he will almost cease to see things: a few lines, a few glimpses, a few simple signs noted in a brief passing glance, will enable him to recognise them; and he will hardly retain any more of reality than its schemes and symbols.

"Perception," says Mr Bergson on this subject, "becomes in the end only an opportunity of recollection."[1]

All concrete perception, it is true, is directed less upon the present than the past. The part of pure perception in it is small, and immediately covered and almost buried by the contribution of memory.

This infinitesimal part acts as a bait. It is a summons to recollection, challenging us to extract from our previous experience, and construct with our acquired wealth a system of images which permits us to read the experience of the moment.

[1] *Matter and Memory*, p. 59.

With our scheme of interpretation thus constituted we encounter the few fugitive traits which we have actually perceived. If the theory we have elaborated adapts itself, and succeeds in accounting for, connecting, and making sense of these traits, we shall finally have a perception properly so called.

Perception then, in the usual sense of the word, is the resolution of a problem, the verification of a theory.

Thus are explained "errors of the senses," which are in reality errors of interpretation. Thus too, and in the same manner, we have the explanation of dreams.

Let us take a simple example. When you read a book, do you spell each syllable, one by one, to group the syllables afterwards into words, and the words into phrases, thus travelling from print to meaning? Not at all: you grasp a few letters accurately, a few downstrokes in their graphical outline; then you guess the remainder, travelling in the reverse direction, from a probable meaning to the print which you are interpreting. This is what causes mistakes in reading, and the well-known difficulty in seeing printing errors.

This observation is confirmed by curious experiments. Write some everyday phrase or other on a blackboard; let there be a few intentional mistakes here and there, a letter or two altered, or left out. Place the words in a dark room in front of a person who, of course, does not know what has been written. Then turn on the light without allowing the observer sufficient time to spell the writing.

In spite of this, he will in most cases read the entire phrase, without hesitation or difficulty.

He has restored what was missing, or corrected what was at fault.

Now, ask him what letters he is certain he saw, and you will find he will tell you an omitted or altered letter as well as a letter actually written.

The observer then thinks he sees in broad light a letter which is not there, if that letter, in virtue of the general sense, ought to appear in the phrase. But you can go further, and vary the experiment.

Suppose we write the word "tumult" correctly. After doing so, to direct the memory of the observer into a certain trend of recollection, call out in his ear, during the short time the light is turned on, another word of different meaning, for example, the word "railway."

The observer will read " tunnel"; that is to say, a word, the graphical outline of which is like that of the written word, but connected in sense with the order of recollection called up.

In this mistake in reading, as in the spontaneous correction of the previous experiment, we see very clearly that perception is always the fulfilment of guesswork.

It is the direction of this work that we are concerned to determine.

According to the popular idea, perception has a completely speculative interest: it is pure knowledge. Therein lies the fundamental mistake.

Notice first of all how much more probable it is, *a priori*, that the work of perception, just as any other natural and spontaneous work, should have a utilitarian signification.

" Life," says Mr Bergson with justice, " is the acceptance from objects of nothing but the *useful* impression, with the response of the appropriate reactions."[1]

And this view receives striking objective confirmation if, with the author of *Matter and Memory*, we follow the progress of the perceptive functions along the animal series from

[1] *Laughter*, p. 154.

the protoplasm to the higher vertebrates ; or if, with him, we analyse the task of the body, and discover that the nervous system is manifested in its very structure as, before all, an instrument of action. Have we not already besides proof of this in the fact that each of us always appears in his own eyes to occupy the centre of the world he perceives?

The *Riquet* of Anatole France voices Mr Bergson's view: " I am always in the centre of everything, and men and beasts and things, for or against me, range themselves around."

But direct analysis leads us still more plainly to the same conclusion.

Let us take the perception of bodies. It is easy to show—and I regret that I cannot here reproduce Mr Bergson's masterly demonstration—that the division of matter into distinct objects with sharp outlines is produced by a selection of images which is completely relative to our practical needs.

" The distinct outlines which we assign to an object, and which bestow upon it its individuality, are nothing but the graph of a certain kind of influence which we should be able to employ at a certain point in space: it is the plan of our future actions which is submitted to our eyes, as in a mirror, when we perceive the surfaces and edges of things. Remove this action, and in consequence the high roads which it makes for itself in advance by perception, in the web of reality, and the individuality of the body will be reabsorbed in the universal interaction which is without doubt reality itself." Which is tantamount to saying that "rough bodies are cut in the material of nature by a *perception* of which the scissors follow, in some sort, the dotted line along which the *action* would pass."[1]

Bodies independent of common experience do not then appear, to an attentive criticism, as veritable realities which would have an existence in themselves. They are only centres of co-ordination for our actions. Or, if you prefer it, "our needs are so many shafts of light which, when played upon the continuity of perceptible qualities, produce in them the outline of distinct bodies."[2] Does not science too, after its own fashion, resolve the atom into a centre of intersecting relations, which finally extend by degrees to the entire universe in an indissoluble interpenetration?

A qualitative continuity, imperceptibly shaded off, over which pass quivers that here

[1] *Creative Evolution*, p. 12.
[2] *Matter and Memory*, p. 220.

and there converge, is the image by which we are forced to recognise a superior degree of reality.

But is this perceptible material, this qualitative continuity, the pure fact in matter? Not yet. Perception, we said just now, is always in reality complicated by memory. There is more truth in this than we had seen. Reality is not a motionless spectrum, extending to our view its infinite shades; it might rather be termed a leaping flame in the spectrum. All is in passage, in process of becoming.

On this flux consciousness concentrates at long intervals, each time condensing into one "quality" an immense period of the inner history of things. "In just this way the thousand successive positions of a runner contract into one single symbolic attitude, which our eye perceives, which art reproduces, and which becomes for everybody the representation of a man running."[1]

In the same way again, a red light, continuing one second, embodies such a large number of elementary pulsations that it would take 25,000 years of our time to see its distinct passage. From here springs the subjectivity

[1] *Matter and Memory*, p. 233.

of our perception. The different qualities correspond, roughly speaking, to the different rhythms of contraction or dilution, to the different degrees of inner tension in the perceiving consciousness.

Pushing the case to its limits, and imagining a complete expansion, matter would resolve into colourless disturbances, and become the "pure matter" of the natural philosopher.

Let us now unite in one single continuity the different periods of the preceding dialectic. Vibration, qualities, and bodies are none of them *reality* by themselves; but all the same they are *part of reality*. And absolute reality would be the whole of these degrees and moments, and many others as well, no doubt. Or rather, to secure absolute intuition of matter, we should have on the one hand to get rid of all that our practical needs have constructed, restore on the other all the effective tendencies they have extinguished, follow the complete scale of qualitative concentrations and dilutions, and pass, by a kind of sympathy, into the incessantly moving play of all the possible innumerable contractions or resolutions; with the result that in the end we should succeed, by a simultaneous view as it were, in grasping, according to their infinitely various modes, the phases of this matter which, though at present latent, admit of "perception."

Thus, in the case before us, *absolute* knowledge is found to be the result of *integral* experience; and though we cannot attain the term, we see at any rate in what direction we should have to work to reach it.

Now it must be stated that our realisable knowledge is at every moment partial and limited rather than exterior and relative, for our effective perception is related to matter in itself as the part to the whole. Our least perceptions are actually based on pure perception, and "we are aware of the elementary disturbances which constitute matter, in the perceptible quality in which they suffer contraction, as we are aware of the beating of our heart in the general feeling that we have of living."[1]

But the preoccupation of practical action, coming between reality and ourselves, produces the fragmentary world of common-sense, much as an absorbing medium resolves into separate rays the continuous spectrum of a luminous body; whilst the rhythm of duration, and the

[1] *The Journal of Philosophy, Psychology, and Scientific Methods,* 7th July 1910.

degree of tension peculiar to our consciousness, limit us to the apprehension of certain qualities only.

What then have we to do to progress towards absolute knowledge? Not to quit experience: quite the contrary; but to extend it and diversify it by science, while, at the same time, by criticism, we correct in it the disturbing effects of action, and finally quicken all the results thus obtained by an effort of sympathy which will make us familiar with the object until we *feel* its profound throbbing and its inner wealth.

In connection with this last vital point, which is decisive, call to mind a celebrated page of Sainte-Beuve where he defines his method: " Enter into your author, make yourself at home in him, produce him under his different aspects, make him live, move, and speak as he must have done; follow him to his fireside and in his domestic habits, as closely as you can. . . .

" Study him, turn him round and round, ask him questions at your leisure; place him before you. . . . Every feature will appear in its turn, and take the place of the man himself in this expression. . . .

" An individual reality will gradually blend

with and become incarnate in the vague, abstract, and general type. . . . There is our man. . . ." Yes, that is exactly what we want: it could not be better put. Transpose this page from the literary to the metaphysical order, and you have intuition, as defined by Mr Bergson. You have the return to immediacy.

But a new problem then arises: Is not our intuition of immediacy in danger of remaining inexpressible? For our language has been formed in view of practical life, not of pure knowledge.

IV

The immediate perception of reality is not all; we have still to translate this perception into intelligible language, into a connected chain of concepts; failing which, it would seem, we should not have knowledge in the strict sense of the word, we should not have truth.

Without language, intuition, supposing it came to birth, would remain intransmissible and incommunicable, and would perish in a solitary cry. By language alone are we enabled to submit it to a positive test: the letter is the ballast of the mind, the body which allows it to act, and in acting to scatter the unreal delusions of dream.

The act of pure intuition demands so great an inner tension from thought that it can only be very rare and very fugitive: a few rapid gleams here and there; and these dawning glimpses must be sustained, and afterwards united, and that again is the work of language.

But while language is thus necessary, no less necessary is a criticism of ordinary language, and of the methods familiar to the understanding. These forms of reflected knowledge, these processes of analysis really convey secretly all the postulates of practical action. But it is imperative that language should translate, not betray; that the body of formulæ should not stifle the soul of intuition. We shall see in what the work of reform and conversion imposed on the philosopher precisely consists.

The attitude of the ordinary proceedings of common thought can be stated in a few words. Place the object studied before yourself as an exterior "thing." Then place yourself outside it, in perspective, at points of vantage on a circumference, whence you can only see the object of your investigation at a distance, with such interval as would be sufficient for the contemplation of a picture; in short, move round the object instead of entering boldly into it. But these proceedings lead to what I shall term analysis by concepts; that is to say, the attempt to resolve all reality into general ideas.

What are concepts and abstract ideas really, but distant and simplified views, species of model drawings, giving only a few summary features of their object, which vary according to direction and angle? By means of them we claim to determine the object from outside, as if, in order to know it, it were sufficient to enclose it in a system of logical sides and angles.

And perhaps in this way we do really grasp it, perhaps we do establish its precise description, but we do not penetrate it.

Concepts translate *relations* resulting from comparisons by which each object is finally expressed as a function of what it is not. They dismember it, divide it up piece by piece, and mount it in various frames. They lay hold of it only by ends and corners, by resemblances and differences. Is not that obviously what is done by the converting theories which explain the soul by the body, life by matter, quality by movements, space itself by pure number? Is not that what is done generally by all criticisms, all doctrines which connect one idea to another, or to a group of other ideas?

In this way we reach only the surface of things, the reciprocal contacts, mutual intersections, and parts common, but not the organic unity nor the inner essence.

In vain we multiply our points of view, our perspectives and plane projections: no accumulation of this kind will reconstruct the concrete solid. We can pass from an object directly perceived to the pictures which represent it, the prints which represent the pictures, the scheme representing the prints, because each stage contains less than the one before, and is obtained from it by simple diminution.

But, inversely, you may take all the schemes, prints, pictures you like—supposing that it is not absurd to conceive as given what is by nature interminable and inexhaustible, lending itself to indefinite enumeration and endless development and multiplicity—but you will never recompose the profound and original unity of the source.

How, by forcing yourself to seek the object outside itself, where it certainly is not, except in echo and reflection, would you ever find its intimate and specific reality? You are but condemning yourself to symbolism, for one "thing" can only be in another symbolically.

To go further still, your knowledge of things will remain irremediably relative, relative to the symbols selected and the points of view adopted. Everything will happen as in a movement of which the appearance and formula vary with the spot from which you regard it, with the marks to which you relate it.

Absolute revelation is only given to the man who passes into the object, flings himself upon its stream, and lives within its rhythm. The thesis which maintains the inevitable relativity of all human knowledge originates mainly from the metaphors employed to describe the act of knowledge. The subject occupies this point, the object that; how are we to span the distance? Our perceptory organs fill the interval; how are we to grasp anything but what reaches us in the receiver at the end of the wire?

The mind itself is a projecting lantern playing a shaft of light on nature; how should it do otherwise than tint nature its own colour?

But these difficulties all arise out of the spatial metaphors employed; and these metaphors in their turn do little but illustrate and translate the common method of analysis by concepts: and this method is essentially regulated by the practical needs of action and language.

The philosopher must adopt an attitude entirely inverse; not keep at a distance from things, but listen in a manner to their inward breathing, and, above all, supply the effort of sympathy by which he establishes himself in the object, becomes on intimate terms with it, tunes himself to its rhythm, and, in a word, lives it. There is really nothing mysterious or strange in this.

Consider your daily judgments in matters of art, profession, or sport.

Between knowledge by theory and knowledge by experience, between understanding by external analogy and perception by profound intuition, what difference and divergence there is!

Who has absolute knowledge of a machine, the student who analyses it in mechanical theorems, or the engineer who has lived in comradeship with it, even to sharing the physical sensation of its laboured or easy working, who feels the play of its inner muscles, its likes and dislikes, who notes its movements and the task before it, as the machine itself would do were it conscious, for whom it has become an extension of his own body, a new sensori-motor organ, a group of prearranged gestures and automatic habits?

The student's knowledge is more useful to the builder, and I do not wish to claim that we should ever neglect it; but the only true knowledge is that of the engineer. And what I have just said does not concern material objects only. Who has absolute knowledge of religion, he who analyses it in psychology, sociology, history, and metaphysics, or he who, from within, by a living experience, participates in its essence and holds communion with its duration?

But the external nature of the knowledge obtained by conceptual analysis is only its least fault. There are others still more serious.

If concepts actually express what is common, general, unspecific, what should make us feel the need of recasting them when we apply them to a new object?

Does not their ground, their utility, and their interest exactly consist in sparing us this labour?

We regard them as elaborated once for all. They are building-material, ready-hewn blocks, which we have only to bring together. They are atoms, simple elements—a mathematician would say prime factors—capable of associating with infinity, but without undergoing any inner modification in contact with it. They admit linkage; they can be attached externally, but they leave the aggregate as they went into it.

Juxtaposition and arrangement are the geometrical operations which typify the work of knowledge in such a case; or else we must fall back on metaphors from some mental chemistry, such as proportioning and combination.

In all cases, the method is still that of alignment and blending of pre-existent concepts.

Now the mere fact of proceeding thus is equivalent to setting up the concept as a symbol of an abstract class. That being done, explanation of a thing is no more than showing it in the intersection of several classes, partaking of each of them in definite proportions: which is the same as considering it sufficiently expressed by a list of general frames into which it will go. The unknown is then, on principle, and in virtue of this theory, referred to the already known; and it thereby becomes impossible ever to grasp any true novelty or any irreducible originality.

On principle, once more, we claim to reconstruct nature with pure symbols; and it thereby becomes impossible ever to reach its concrete reality, "the invisible and present soul."

This intuitional coinage in fixed standard concepts, this creation of an easily handled intellectual cash, is no doubt of evident practical utility. For knowledge in the usual sense of the word is not a disinterested operation; it consists in finding out what profit we can draw from an object, how we are to conduct ourselves towards it, what label we can suitably attach to it, under what already known class it comes, to what degree it is deserving of this or that title which determines an attitude we must take up, or a step we must perform. Our end is to place the object in its approximate class, having regard to advantageous employment or to everyday language. Then, and only then, we find our pigeon-holes all ready-made; and the same parcel of reagents meets all cases. A universal catechism is here in existence to meet every research; its different clauses define so many unshifting points of view, from which we

46   A NEW PHILOSOPHY

regard each object, and our study is subsequently limited to applying a kind of nomenclature to the preconstructed frames.

Once again the philosopher has to proceed in exactly the opposite direction. He has not to confine himself to ready-made business concepts, of the ordinary kind, suits cut to an average model, which fit nobody because they almost fit everybody; but he has to work to measure, incessantly renew his plant, continually recreate his mind, and meet each new problem with a fresh adaptive effort. He must not go from concepts to things, as if each of them were only the cutting-point of several concurrent generalities, an ideal centre of intersecting abstractions; on the contrary, he must go from things to concepts, incessantly creating new thoughts, and incessantly recasting the old.

There could be no solution of the problem in a more or less ingenious mosaic or tessellation of rigid concepts, pre-existing to be employed. We need plastic fluid, supple and living concepts, capable of being continually modelled on reality, of delicately following its infinite curves. The philosopher's task is then to create concepts much more than to combine them. And each of the concepts he creates must remain open and adjustable, ready for the necessary renewal and adaptation, like a method or a programme: it must be the arrow pointing to a path which descends from intuition to language, not a boundary marking a terminus. In this way only does philosophy remain what it ought to be: the examination into the consciousness of the human mind, the effort towards enlargement and depth which it attempts unremittingly, in order to advance beyond its present intellectual condition.

Do you want an example? I will take that of human personality. The *ego* is one; the *ego* is many: no one contests this double formula. But everything admits of it; and what is its lesson to us? Observe what is bound to happen to the two concepts of unity and multiplicity, by the mere fact that we take them for general frames independent of the reality contained, for detached language admitting empty and blank definition, always representable by the same word, no matter what the circumstances: they are no longer living and coloured ideas, but abstract, motionless, and neutral forms, without shades or gradations, without distinction of case, characterising two points of view from which you can observe anything and everything.

48 A NEW PHILOSOPHY

This being so, how could the application of these forms help us to grasp the original and peculiar nature of the unity and multiplicity of the ego? Still further, how could we, between two such entities, statically defined by their opposition, ever imagine a synthesis? Correctly speaking, the interesting question is not whether *there is* unity, multiplicity, combination, one with the other, but to see *what sort* of unity, multiplicity, or combination realises the case in point; above all, to understand *how* the living person is at once multiple unity and one multiplicity, *how* these two poles of conceptual dissociation are connected, *how* these two diverging branches of abstraction join at the roots. The interesting point, in a word, is not the two symbolical colourless marks indicating the two ends of the spectrum; it is the continuity between, with its changing wealth of colouring, and the double progress of shades which resolve it into red and violet.

But it is impossible to arrive at this concrete transition unless we begin from direct intuition and descend to the analysing concepts.

Again, the same duty of reversing our familiar attitude, of inverting our customary proceeding, becomes ours for another reason.

METHOD

The conceptual atomism of common thought leads it to place movement in a lower order than rest, fact in a lower order than becoming. According to common thought, movement is added to the atom, as a supplementary accident to a body previously at rest; and, by becoming, the pre-existent terms are strung together like pearls on a necklace. It delights in rest, and endeavours to bring to rest all that moves. Immobility appears to it to be the base of existence. It decomposes and pulverises every change and every phenomenon, until it finds the invariable element in them. It is immobility which it esteems as primary, fundamental, intelligible of itself; and motion, on the contrary, which it seeks to explain as a function of immobility. And so it tends, out of progresses and transitions, to make things. To see distinctly, it appears to need a dead halt. What indeed are concepts but logical look-out stations along the path of becoming? what are they but motionless external views, taken at intervals, of an uninterrupted stream of movement?

Each of them isolates and fixes an aspect, "as the instantaneous lightning flashes on a storm-scene in the darkness."[1]

[1] *Matter and Memory*, p. 209.

50   A NEW PHILOSOPHY

Placed together, they make a net laid in advance, a strong meshwork in which the human intelligence posts itself securely to spy the flux of reality, and seize it as it passes. Such a proceeding is made for the practical world, and is out of place in the speculative. Everywhere we are trying to find *constants*, identities, non-variants, states; and we imagine ideal science as an open eye which gazes for ever upon objects that do not move. The constant is the concrete support demanded by our action: the matter upon which we operate must not escape our grasp and slip through our hands, if we are to be able to work it. The constant, again, is the element of language, in which the word represents its inert permanence, in which it constitutes the solid fulcrum, the foundation and landmark of dialectic progress, being that which can be discarded by the mind, whose attention is thus free for other tasks. In this respect analysis by concepts is the natural method of common-sense. It consists in asking from time to time what point the object studied has reached, what it has become, in order to see what one could derive from it, or what it is fitting to say of it.

But this method has only a practical reach. Reality, which in its essence is becoming, passes through our concepts without ever letting itself be caught, as a moving body passes fixed points. When we filter it, we retain only its deposit, the result of the becoming drifted down to us.

Do the dams, canals, and buoys make the current of the river? Do the festoons of dead seaweed ranged along the sand make the rising tide? Let us beware of confounding the stream of becoming with the sharp outline of its result. Analysis by concepts is a cinematograph method, and it is plain that the inner organisation of the movement is not seen in the moving pictures. Every moment we have fixed views of moving objects. With such conceptual sections taken in the stream of continuity, however many we accumulate, should we ever reconstruct the movement itself, the dynamic connection, the march of the images, the transition from one view to another? This capacity for movement must be contained in the picture apparatus, and must therefore be given in addition to the views themselves; and nothing can better prove how, after all, movement is never explicable except by itself, never grasped except in itself.

But if we take movement as our principle,

it is, on the contrary, possible, and even easy, to slacken speed by imperceptible degrees, and stop dead.

From a dead stop we shall never get our movement again; but rest can very well be conceived as the limit of movement, as its arrest or extinction; for rest is *less* than movement.

In this way the true philosophical method, which is the inverse of the common method, consists in taking up a position from the very outset in the bosom of becoming, in adopting its changing curves and variable tension, in sympathising with the rhythm of its genesis, in perceiving all existence from within, as a growth, in following it in its inner generation; in short, in promoting movement to fundamental reality, and, inversely, in degrading fixed states to the rank of secondary and derived reality.

And thus, to come back to the example of the human personality, the philosopher must seek in the ego not so much a ready-made unity or multiplicity as, if I may venture the expression, two antagonistic and correlative movements of *unification* and *plurification*.

There is then a radical difference between philosophic intuition and conceptual analysis.

METHOD 53

The latter delights in the play of dialectic, in fountains of knowledge, where it is interested only in the immovable basins; the former goes back to the source of the concepts, and seeks to possess it where it gushes out. Analysis cuts the channels; intuition supplies the water. Intuition acquires and analysis expends.

It is not a question of banning analysis; science could not do without it, and philosophy could not do without science. But we must reserve for it its normal place and its just task.

Concepts are the deposited sediment of intuition: intuition produces the concepts, not the concepts intuition. From the heart of intuition you will have no difficulty in seeing how it splits up and analyses into concepts, concepts of such and such a kind or such and such a shade. But by successive analyses you will never reconstruct the least intuition, just as, no matter how you distribute the water, you will never reconstruct the reservoir in its original condition.

Begin from intuition: it is a summit from which we can descend by infinite slopes; it is a picture which we can place in an infinite number of frames. But all the frames together will not recompose the picture, and the lower ends of all the slopes will not explain how they

54 A NEW PHILOSOPHY

meet at the summit. Intuition is a necessary beginning; it is the impulse which sets the analysis in motion, and gives it direction; it is the sounding which brings it to solid bottom; the soul which assures its unity. "I shall never understand how black and white interpenetrate, if I have not seen grey, but I understand without trouble, after once seeing grey, how we can regard it from the double point of view of black and white."[1]

Here are some letters which you can arrange in chains in a thousand ways: the indivisible sense running along the chain, and making one phrase of it, is the original cause of the writing, not its consequence. Thus it is with intuition in relation to analysis. But beginnings and generative activities are the proper object of the philosopher. Thus the conversion and reform incumbent on him consist essentially in a transition from the analytic to the intuitive point of view.

The result is that the chosen instrument of philosophic thought is metaphor; and of metaphor we know Mr Bergson to be an incomparable master. What we have to do, he says himself, is "to elicit a certain active force which in most men is liable to be trammelled

[1] *Introduction to Metaphysics.*

by mental habits more useful to life," to awaken in them the feeling of the immediate, original, and concrete. But "many different images, borrowed from very different orders of things, can, by their convergent action, direct consciousness to the precise point where there is a certain intuition to be seized. By choosing images as unlike as possible, we prevent any one of them from usurping the place of the intuition it is intended to call up, since it would in that case be immediately routed by its rivals. In making them all, despite their different aspects, demand of our mind the same kind of attention, and in some way the same degree of tension, we accustom our consciousness little by little to a quite peculiar and well-determined disposition, precisely the one which it ought to adopt to appear to itself unmasked."[1]

Strictly speaking, the intuition of immediacy is inexpressible. But it can be suggested and called up. How? By ringing it round with concurrent metaphors. Our aim is to modify the habits of imagination in ourselves which are opposed to a simple and direct view, to break through the mechanical imagery in which we have allowed ourselves to be caught;

[1] *Introduction to Metaphysics.*

56   A NEW PHILOSOPHY

and it is by awakening other imagery and other habits that we can succeed in so doing.

But then, you will say, where is the difference between philosophy and art, between metaphysical and æsthetic intuition? Art also tends to reveal nature to us, to suggest to us a direct vision of it, to lift the veil of illusion which hides us from ourselves; and æsthetic intuition is, in its own way, perception of immediacy. We revive the feeling of reality obliterated by habit, we summon the deep and penetrating soul of things: the object is the same in both cases; and the means are also the same; images and metaphors. Is Mr Bergson only a poet, and does his work amount to nothing but the introduction of impressionism in metaphysics?

It is an old objection. If the truth be told, Mr Bergson's immense scientific knowledge should be sufficient refutation.

Only those who have not read the mass of carefully proved and positive discussions could give way thus to the impressions of art awakened by what is truly a magic style. But we can go further and put it better.

That there are analogies between philosophy and art, between metaphysical and æsthetic intuition, is unquestionable and uncontested.

At the same time, the analogies must not be allowed to hide the differences.

Art is, to a certain extent, philosophy previous to analysis, previous to criticism and science; the æsthetic intuition is metaphysical intuition in process of birth, bounded by dream, not proceeding to the test of positive verification. Reciprocally, philosophy is the art which follows upon science, and takes account of it, the art which uses the results of analysis as its material, and submits itself to the demands of stern criticism; metaphysical intuition is the æsthetic intuition verified, systematised, ballasted by the language of reason.

Philosophy then differs from art in two essential points: first of all, it rests upon, envelops, and supposes science; secondly, it implies a test of verification in its strict meaning. Instead of stopping at the acts of common-sense, it completes them with all the contributions of analysis and scientific investigation.

We said just now of common-sense that, in its inmost depths, it possesses reality: that is only quite exact when we mean common-sense developed in positive science; and that is why philosophy takes the results of science as its basis, for each of these results, like the facts and data of common perception, opens a way for critical penetration towards the immediate. Just now I was comparing the two kinds of knowledge which the theorist and the engineer can have of a machine, and I allowed the advantage of absolute knowledge to practical experience, whilst theory seemed to me mainly relative to the constructive industry. That is true, and I do not go back upon it. But the most experienced engineer, who did not know the mechanism of his machine, who possessed only unanalysed feelings about it, would have only an artist's, not a philosopher's knowledge. For absolute intuition, in the full sense of the word, we must have integral experience; that is to say, a living application of rational theory no less than of working technique.

To journey towards living intuition, starting from complete science and complete sensation, is the philosopher's task; and this task is governed by standards unknown to art.

Metaphysical intuition offers a victorious resistance to the test of thorough and continued experiment, to the test of calculation as to that of working, to the complete experiment which brings into play all the various deoxidising agents of criticism; it shows itself capable of withstanding analysis without dissolving or succumbing; it abounds in concepts which satisfy the understanding, and exalt it; in a word, it creates light and truth on all mental planes; and these characteristics are sufficient to distinguish it in a profound degree from æsthetic intuition.

The latter is only the prophetic type of the former, a dream or presentiment, a veiled and still uncertain dawn, a twilight myth preceding and proclaiming, in the half-darkness, the full day of positive revelation. . . .

Every philosophy has two faces, and must be studied in two movements—method and teaching.

These are its two moments, its two aspects, no doubt co-ordinate and mutually dependent, but none the less distinct.

We have just examined the method of the new philosophy inaugurated by Mr Bergson. To what teaching has this method led us, and to what can we foresee that it will lead us?

This is what we have still to find.

II
TEACHING

THE sciences properly so called, those that are by agreement termed positive, present themselves as so many external and circumferential points from which we view reality. They leave us on the outside of things, and confine themselves to investigating from a distance.

The views they give us resemble the brief perspectives of a town which we obtain in looking at it from different angles on the surrounding hills.

Less even than that: for very soon, by increasing abstraction, the coloured views give place to regular lines, and even to simple conventional notes, which are more practical in use and waste less time. And so the sciences remain prisoners of the symbol, and all the inevitable relativity involved in its use. But philosophy claims to pierce within reality, establish itself in the object, follow its thousand turns and folds, obtain from it a direct and immediate feeling, and penetrate right into the concrete depths of its heart; it is not content with an analysis, but demands an intuition.

Now there is one existence which, at the outset, we know better and more surely than any other; there is a privileged case in which the effort of sympathetic revelation is natural and almost easy to us; there is one reality at least which we grasp from within, which we perceive in its deep and internal content. This reality is ourselves. It is typical of all reality, and our study may fitly begin here. Psychology puts us in direct contact with it, and metaphysics attempt to generalise this contact. But such a generalisation can only be attempted if, to begin with, we are familiar with reality at the point where we have immediate access to it.

The path of thought which the philosopher must take is from the inner to the outer being.

I

"Know thyself": the old maxim has remained the motto of philosophy since Socrates, the motto at least which marks its initial moment, when, inclining towards the depth of the subject, it commences its true work of penetration, whilst science continues to extend on the surface. Each philosophy in turn has commented upon and applied this old motto. But Mr Bergson, more than anyone else, has given it, as he does everything else he takes up, a new and profound meaning. What was the current interpretation before him? Speaking only of the last century, we may say that, under the influence of Kant, criticism had till now been principally engaged in unravelling the contribution of the subject in the act of consciousness, in establishing our perception of things through certain representative forms borrowed from our own constitution. Such was, even yesterday, the authenticated way of regarding the problem. And it is precisely this attitude which Mr Bergson, by a volte-face which will remain familiar to him in the course of his researches, reverses from the outset.

"It has appeared to me," says he,[1] "that there was ground for setting oneself the inverse problem, and asking whether the most apparent states of the ego itself, which we think we grasp directly, are not most of the time perceived through certain forms borrowed from

[1] *Essay on the Immediate Data of Consciousness*, Conclusion.

the outer world, which in this way gives us back what we have lent it. *A priori*, it seems fairly probable that this is what goes on. For supposing that the forms of which we are speaking, to which we adapt matter, come entirely from the mind, it seems difficult to apply them constantly to objects without soon producing the colouring of the objects in the forms; therefore in using these forms for the knowledge of our own personality, we risk taking a reflection of the frame in which we place them—that is, actually, the external world—for the very colouring of the ego. But we can go further, and state that forms applicable to things cannot be entirely our own work; that they must result from a compromise between matter and mind; that if we give much to this matter, we doubtless receive something from it; and that, in this way, when we try to possess ourselves again after an excursion into the outer world, we no longer have our hands free."

To avoid such a consequence, there is, we must admit, a conceivable loophole. It consists in maintaining on principle an absolute analogy, an exact similitude between internal reality and external objects. The forms which suit the one would then also suit the other.

But it must be observed that such a principle constitutes in the highest degree a metaphysical thesis which it would be on all hands illegal to assert previously as a postulate of method. Secondly, and above all, it must be observed that on this head experience is decisive, and manifests more plainly every day the failure of the theories which try to assimilate the world of consciousness to that of matter, to copy psychology from physics. We have here two different "orders." The apparatus of the first does not admit of being employed in the second. Hence the necessity of the attitude adopted by Mr Bergson. We have an effort to make, a work of reform to undertake, to lift the veil of symbols which envelops our usual representation of the ego, and thus conceals us from our own view, in order to find out what we are in reality, immediately, in our inmost selves. This effort and this work are necessary, because, "in order to contemplate the ego in its original purity, psychology must eliminate or correct certain forms which bear the visible mark of the outer world."[1] What are these forms? Let us confine ourselves to the most important. Things appear to us as numerable units, placed side by side in space.

[1] *Essay on the Immediate Data of Consciousness*, Conclusion.

They compose numerical and spatial multiplicity, a dust of terms between which geometrical ties are established.

But space and number are the two forms of immobility, the two schemes of analysis, by which we must not let ourselves be obsessed. I do not say that there is no place to give them, even in the internal world. But the more deeply we enter into the heart of psychological life, the less they are in place.

The fact is, there are several *planes of consciousness*, situated at different depths, marking all the intervening degrees between pure thought and bodily action, and each mental phenomenon interests all these planes simultaneously, and is thus repeated in a thousand higher tones, like the harmonies of one and the same note.

Or, if you prefer it, the life of the spirit is not the uniform transparent surface of a mere; rather it is a gushing spring which, at first pent in, spreads upwards and outwards, like a sheaf of corn, passing through many different states, from the dark and concentrated welling of the source to the gleam of the scattered tumbling spray; and each of its moods presents in its turn a similar character, being itself only a thread within the whole. Such without doubt is the central and activating idea of the admirable book entitled *Matter and Memory*. I cannot possibly condense its substance here, or convey its astonishing synthetic power, which succeeds in contracting a complete metaphysic, and in gripping it so firmly that the examination ends by passing to the discussion of a few humble facts relative to the philosophy of the brain! But its technical severity and its very conciseness, combined with the wealth it contains, render it irresumable; and I can only in a few words indicate its conclusions.

First of all, however little we pride ourselves on positive method, we must admit the existence of an internal world, of a spiritual activity distinct from matter and its mechanism. No chemistry of the brain, no dance of atoms, is equivalent to the least thought, or indeed to the least sensation.

Some, it is true, have brought forward a thesis of parallelism, according to which each mental phenomenon corresponds point by point to a phenomenon in the brain, without adding anything to it, without influencing its course, merely translating it into another tongue, so that a glance sufficiently penetrating to follow the molecular revolutions and the fluxes of nervous production in their least episodes would immediately read the inmost secrets of the associated consciousness.

But no one will deny that a thesis of this kind is only in reality a hypothesis, that it goes enormously beyond the certain data of current biology, and that it can only be formulated by anticipating future discoveries in a preconceived direction. Let us be candid: it is not really a thesis of positive science, but a metaphysical thesis in the unpleasant meaning of the term. Taking it at its best, its worth to-day could only be one of intelligibleness. And intelligible it is not.

How are we to understand a consciousness destitute of activity and consequently without connection with reality, a kind of phosphorescence which emphasises the lines of vibration in the brain, and renders in miraculous duplicate, by its mysterious and useless light, certain phenomena already complete without it?

One day Mr Bergson came down into the arena of dialectic, and, talking to his opponents in their own language, pulled their "psychophysiological paralogism" to pieces before their eyes; it is only by confounding in one and the same argument two systems of incompatible notations, idealism and realism, that we succeed in enunciating the parallelist thesis. This reasoning went home, all the more as it was adapted to the usual form of discussions between philosophers. But a more positive and more categorical proof is to be found all through *Matter and Memory*. From the precise example of recollection analysed to its lowest depths, Mr Bergson completely grasps and measures the divergence between soul and body, between mind and matter. Then, putting into practice what he said elsewhere about the creation of new concepts, he arrives at the conclusion — these are his own expressions — that between the psychological fact and its counterpart in the brain there must be a relation *sui generis*, which is neither the determination of the one by the other, nor their reciprocal independence, nor the production of the latter by the former, nor of the former by the latter, nor their simple parallel concomitance; in short, a relation which answers to none of the ready-made concepts which abstraction puts at our service, but which may be approximately formulated in these terms:[1]

"Given a psychological state, that part of

[1] *Report of the French Philosophical Society,* meeting, 2nd May 1901.

the state which admits of *play*, the part which would be translated by an attitude of the body or by bodily actions, is represented in the brain ; the remainder is independent of it, and has no equivalent in the brain. So that to one and the same state of the brain there may be many different psychological states which correspond, though not all kinds of states. They are psychological states which all have in common the same *motor scheme*. Into one and the same frame many pictures may go, but not all pictures. Let us take a lofty abstract philosophical thought. We do not conceive it without adding to it an image representing it, which we place beneath.

"We do not represent the image to ourselves, again, without supporting it by a design which resumes its leading features. We do not imagine this design itself without imagining and, in so doing, sketching certain movements which would reproduce it. It is this sketch, and this sketch only, which is represented in the brain. Frame the sketch, there is a margin for the image. Frame the image again, there remains a margin, and a still larger margin, for the thought. The thought is thus relatively free and indeterminate in relation to the activity which conditions it in the brain, for this activity expresses only the motive articulation of the idea, and the articulation may be the same for ideas absolutely different. And yet it is not complete liberty nor absolute indetermination, since any kind of idea, taken at hazard, would not present the articulation desired.

"In short, none of the simple concepts furnished us by philosophy could express the relation we seek, but this relation appears with tolerable clearness to result from experiment."

The same analysis of facts tells us how the planes of consciousness, of which I spoke just now, are arranged, the law by which they are distributed, and the meaning which attaches to their disposition. Let us neglect the intervening multiples, and look only at the extreme poles of the series.

We are inclined to imagine too abrupt a severance between gesture and dream, between action and thought, between body and mind. There are not two plane surfaces, without thickness or transition, placed one above the other on different levels; it is by an imperceptible degradation of increasing depth, and decreasing materiality, that we pass from one term to the other.

TEACHING 71

And the characteristics are continually changing in the course of the transition. Thus our initial problem confronts us again, more acutely than ever: are the forms of number and space equally suitable on all planes of consciousness?

Let us consider the most external of these planes of life, the one which is in contact with the outer world, the one which receives directly the impressions of external reality. We live as a rule on the surface of ourselves, in the numerical and spatial dispersion of language and gesture. Our deeper *ego* is covered as it were with a tough crust, hardened in action: it is a skein of motionless and numerable habits, side by side, and of distinct and solid things, with sharp outlines and mechanical relations. And it is for the representation of the phenomena which occur within this dead rind that space and number are valid.

For we have to live, I mean live our common daily life, with our body, with our customary mechanism rather than with our true depths. Our attention is therefore most often directed by a natural inclination to the practical worth and useful function of our internal states, to the public object of which they are the sign, to the effect they produce externally, to the gestures by which we express them in space. A social average of individual modalities interests us more than the incommunicable originality of our deeper life. The words of language besides offer us so many symbolic centres round which crystallise groups of motor mechanisms set up by habit, the only usual elements of our internal determinations. Now, contact with society has rendered these motor mechanisms practically identical in all men. Hence, whether it be a question of sensation, feeling, or ideas, we have these neutral dry and colourless residua, which spread lifeless over the surface of ourselves, "like dead leaves on the water of a pond."[1]

Thus the *progress* we have lived falls into the rank of a *thing* that can be handled. Space and number lay hold of it. And soon all that remains of what was movement and life is combinations formed and annulled, and forces mechanically composed in a whole of juxtaposed atoms, and to represent this whole a collection of petrified concepts, manipulated in dialectic like counters.

Quite different appears the true inner reality, and quite different are its profound characteristics. To begin with, it contains nothing

[1] *Essay on the Immediate Data,* p. 102.

quantitative; the intensity of a psychological state is not a magnitude, nor can it be measured. The *Essay on the Immediate Data of Consciousness* begins with the proof of this leading statement. If it is a question of a simple state, such as a sensation of light or weight, the intensity is measured by a certain quality of shade which indicates to us approximately, by an association of ideas and thanks to our acquired experience, the magnitude of the objective cause from which it proceeds. If, on the contrary, it is a question of a complex state, such as those impressions of profound joy or sorrow which lay hold of us entirely, invading and overwhelming us, what we call their intensity expresses only the confused feeling of a qualitative progress, and increasing wealth. "Take, for example, an obscure desire, which has gradually become a profound passion. You will see that the feeble intensity of this desire consisted first of all in the fact that it seemed to you isolated and in a way foreign to all the rest of your inner life. But little by little it penetrated a larger number of psychic elements, dyeing them, so to speak, its own colour; and now you find your point of view on things as a whole appears to you to have changed. Is it not true that you become aware of a profound passion, once it has taken root, by the fact that the same objects no longer produce the same impression upon you? All your sensations, all your ideas, appear to you refreshed by it; it is like a new childhood."[1]

There is here none of the homogeneity which is the property of magnitude, and the necessary condition of measurement, giving a view of the *less* in the bosom of the *more*. The element of number has vanished, and with it numerical multiplicity extended in space. Our inner states form a qualitative continuity; they are prolonged and blended into one another; they are grouped in harmonies, each note of which contains an echo of the whole; they are encircled by an innumerable degradation of halos, which gradually colour the total content of consciousness; they live each in the bosom of his fellow.

"I am the scent of roses," were the words Condillac put in the mouth of his statue; and these words translate the immediate truth exactly, as soon as observation becomes naïve and simple enough to attain pure fact. In a passing breath I breathe my childhood; in the rustle of leaves, in a ray of moonlight, I find

[1] *Loc. cit.*, p. 6.

an infinite series of reflections and dreams. A thought, a feeling, an act, may reveal a complete soul. My ideas, my sensations, are like me. How would such facts be possible, if the multiple unity of the *ego* did not present the essential characteristic of vibrating in its entirety in the depths of each of the parts descried or rather determined in it by analysis? All psychical determinations envelop and imply each other reciprocally. And the fact that the soul is thus present in its entirety in each of its acts, its feelings, for example, or its ideas in its sensations, its recollections in its percepts, its inclinations in its obvious states, is the justifying principle of metaphors, the source of all poetry, the truth which modern philosophy proclaims with more force every day under the name of immanence of thought, the fact which explains our moral responsibility with regard to our affections and our beliefs themselves; and finally, it is the best of us, since it is this which ensures our being able to surrender ourselves, genuinely and unreservedly, and this which constitutes the real unity of our person.

Let us push still further into the hidden retreat of the soul. Here we are in these regions of twilight and dream, where our *ego* takes shape, where the spring within us gushes up, in the warm secrecy of the darkness which ushers our trembling being into birth. Distinctions fail us. Words are useless now. We hear the wells of consciousness at their mysterious task like an invisible shiver of running water through the mossy shadow of the caves. I dissolve in the joy of becoming. I abandon myself to the delight of being a pulsing reality. I no longer know whether I see scents, breathe sounds, or smell colours. Do I love? Do I think? The question has no longer a meaning for me. I am, in my complete self, each of my attitudes, each of my changes. It is not my sight which is indistinct or my attention which is idle. It is I who have resumed contact with pure reality, whose essential movement admits no form of number. He who thus makes the really "deep" and "inner" effort necessary to becoming—were it only for an elusive moment—discovers, under the simplest appearance, inexhaustible sources of unsuspected wealth; the rhythm of his duration becomes amplified and refined; his acts become more conscious; and in what seemed to him at first sudden severance or instantaneous pulsation he discovers complex transitions imperceptibly shaded off, musical transitions full of unexpected repetitions and threaded movements.

Thus, the deeper we go in consciousness, the less suitable become these schemes of separation and fixity existing in spatial and numerical forms. The inner world is that of pure quality. There is no measurable homogeneity, no collection of atomically constructed elements. The phenomena distinguished in it by analysis are not composing units, but phases. And it is only when they reach the surface, when they come in contact with the external world, when they are incarnated in language or gesture, that the categories of matter become adapted to them. In its true nature, reality appears as an uninterrupted flow, an impalpable shiver of fluid changing tones, a perpetual flux of waves which ebb and break and dissolve into one another without shock or jar. Everything is ceaseless change; and the state which appears the most stable is already change, since it continues and grows old. Constant quantities are represented only by the materialisation of habit or by means of practical symbols. And it is on this point that Mr Bergson rightly insists.[1]

"The apparent discontinuity of psycho-

[1] *Creative Evolution*, p. 3.

logical life is due, then, to the fact that our attention is concentrated on it in a series of discontinuous acts; where there is only a gentle slope, we think we see, when we follow the broken line of our attention, the steps of a staircase. It is true that our psychological life is full of surprises. A thousand incidents arise which seem to contrast with what precedes them, and not to be connected with what follows. But the gap in their appearances stands out against the continuous background on which they are represented, and to which they owe the very intervals that separate them; they are the drumbeats which break into the symphony at intervals. Our attention is fixed upon them because they interest it more, but each of them proceeds from the fluid mass of our entire psychological existence. Each of them is only the brightest point in a moving zone which understands all that we feel, think, wish; in fact, all that we are at a given moment. It is this zone which really constitutes our state. But we may observe that states defined in this way are not distinct elements. They are an endless stream of mutual continuity."

And do not think that perhaps such a description represents only or principally our life of feeling. Reason and thought share the same characteristic, as soon as we penetrate their living depth, whether it be a question of creative invention or of those primordial judgments which direct our activity. If they evidence greater stability, it is in permanence of direction, because our past remains present to us.

For we are endowed with memory, and that perhaps is, on the whole, our most profound characteristic. It is by memory we enlarge ourselves and draw continually upon the wealth of our treasuries. Hence comes the completely original nature of the change which constitutes us. But it is here that we must shake off familiar representations! Commonsense cannot think in terms of movement. It forges a static conception of it, and destroys it by arresting it under pretext of seeing it better. To define movement as a series of positions, with a generating law, with a time-table or correspondence sheet between places and times, is surely a ready-made presentation. Are we not confusing the trajectory and its performance, the points traversed and the traversing of the points, the result of the genesis and the genesis of the result; in short, the quantitative distance over which the flight extends, and the qualitative flight which puts this distance behind it? In this way the very mobility which is the essence of movement vanishes. There is the same common mistake about time. Analytic and synthetic thought can see in time only a string of coincidences, each of them instantaneous, a logical series of relations. It imagines the whole of it to be a graduated slide-rule, in which the luminous point called the present is the geometrical index.

Thus it gives form to time in space, "a kind of fourth dimension,"[1] or at least it reduces it to nothing more than an abstract scheme of succession, "a stream without bottom or sides, flowing without determinable strength, in an indefinable direction."[2] It requires time to be homogeneous, and every homogeneous medium is space, "for as homogeneity consists here in the absence of any quality, it is not clear how two forms of homogeneity could be distinguished one from the other."[3]

Quite different appears real duration, the duration which is lived. It is pure hetero-

[1] *Essay on the Immediate Data.*
[2] *Introduction to Metaphysics.*
[3] *Essay on the Immediate Data*, p. 74.

geneity. It contains a thousand different degrees of tension or relaxation, and its rhythm varies without end. The magic silence of calm nights or the wild disorder of a tempest, the still joy of ecstasy or the tumult of passion unchained, a steep climb towards a difficult truth or a gentle descent from a luminous principle to consequences which easily follow, a moral crisis or a shooting pain, call up intuitions admitting no comparison with one another. We have here no series of moments, but prolonged and interpenetrating phases; their sequence is not a substitution of one point for another, but rather resembles a musical resolution of harmony into harmony. And of this ever-new melody which constitutes our inner life every moment contains a resonance or an echo of past moments. "What are we really, what is our character, except the condensation of the history which we have lived since our birth, even before our birth, since we bring with us our prenatal dispositions? Without doubt we think only with a small part of our past; but it is with our complete past, including our original bias of soul, that we desire, wish, and act."[1] This is what makes our duration irreversible, and its

[1] *Creative Evolution*, pp. 5-6.

novelty perpetual, for each of the states through which it passes envelops the recollection of all past states. And thus we see, in the end, how, for a being endowed with memory, "existence consists in change, change in ripening, ripening in endless self-creation."[1]

With this formula we face the capital problem in which psychology and metaphysics meet, that of liberty. The solution given by Mr Bergson marks one of the culminating points of his philosophy. It is from this summit that he finds light thrown on the riddle of inner being. And it is the centre where all the lines of his research converge.

What is liberty? What must we understand by this word? Beware of the answer you are going to give. Every definition, in the strict sense of the term, will imply the determinist thesis in advance, since, under pain of going round in a circle, it will be bound to express liberty as a function of what it is not. Either psychological liberty is an illusive appearance, or, if it is real, we can only grasp it by intuition, not by analysis, in the light of an immediate feeling. For a reality is verified, not constructed; and we are now or never in one of those situations where the philosopher's

[1] *Creative Evolution,* p. 8.

task is to create some new concept, instead of abiding by a combination of previous elements.

Man is free, says common-sense, in so far as his action depends only on himself. "We are free," says Mr Bergson,[1] "when our acts proceed from our entire personality, when they express it, when they exhibit that indefinable resemblance to it which we find occasionally between the artist and his work." That is all we need seek; two conceptions which are equivalent to each other, two concordant formulæ. It is true that this amounts to determining the free act by its very *originality*, in the etymological sense of the word: which is at bottom only another way of declaring it incommensurable with every concept, and reluctant to be confined by any definition. But, after all, is not that the only true immediate fact?

That our spiritual life is genuine action, capable of independence, initiative, and irreducible novelty, not mere result produced from outside, not simple extension of external mechanism, that it is so much ours as to constitute every moment, for him who can see, an essentially incomparable and new

[1] *Essay on the Immediate Data of Consciousness*, p. 131.

invention, is exactly what represents for us the name of liberty. Understood thus, and decidedly it is like this that we must understand it, liberty is a profound thing: we seek it only in those moments of high and solemn choice which come into our life, not in the petty familiar actions which their very insignificance submits to all surrounding influences, to every wandering breeze. Liberty is rare; many live and die and have never known it. Liberty is a thing which contains an infinite number of degrees and shades; it is measured by our capacity for the inner life. Liberty is a thing which goes on in us unceasingly: our liberty is potential rather than actual. And lastly, it is a thing of duration, not of space and number, not the work of moments or decrees. The free act is the act which has been long in preparing, the act which is heavy with our whole history, and falls like a ripe fruit from our past life.

But how are we to establish positive verification of these views? How are we to do away with the danger of illusion? The proof will in this case result from a criticism of adverse theories, along with direct observation of psychological reality freed from the deceptive forms which warp the common perception of it. And it will here be an easy task to resume Mr Bergson's reasoning in a few words.

The first obstacle which confronts affirmation of our liberty comes from physical determinism. Positive science, we are told, presents the universe to us as an immense homogeneous transformation, maintaining an exact equivalence between departure and arrival. How can we possibly have after that the genuine creation which we require in the act we call free?

The answer is that the universality of the mechanism is at bottom only a hypothesis which is still awaiting demonstration. On the one hand it includes the parallelist conception which we have recognised as effete. And on the other it is plain that it is not self-sufficient. At least it requires that somewhere or other there should be a principle of position giving once for all what will afterwards be maintained. In actual fact, the course of phenomena displays three tendencies: a tendency to conservation, beyond question; but also a tendency to collapse, as in the diminution of energy; and a tendency to progress, as in biological evolution. To make conservation the sole law of matter implies an arbitrary decree, denoting only those aspects of reality which will count for anything. By what right do we thus exclude, with vital effort, even the feeling of liberty which in us is so vigorous?

We might say, it is true, that our spiritual life, if it is not a simple extension of external mechanism, yet proceeds according to an internal mechanism equally severe, but of a different order. This would bring us to the hypothesis of a kind of psychological mechanism; and in many respects this seems to be the common-sense hypothesis. I need not dwell upon it, after the numerous criticisms already made. Inner reality—which does not admit number —is not a sequence of distinct terms, allowing a disconnected waste of absolute causality.

And the mechanism of which we dream has no true sense—for, after all, it has a sense— except in relation to the superficial phenomena which take place in our dead rind, in relation to the automaton which we are in daily life. I am ready to admit that it explains our common actions, but here it is our profound consciousness which is in question, not the play of our materialised habits.

Without insisting, then, too strongly on this mongrel conception, let us pass to the direct examination of inner psychological reality.

Everything is ready for the conclusion. Our duration, which is continually accumulating itself, and always introducing some irreducible new factor, prevents any kind of state, even if superficially identical, from repeating itself in depth. "We shall never again have the soul we had this evening." Each of our moments remains essentially unique. It is something new added to the surviving past; not only new, but unable to be foreseen.

For how can we speak of foresight which is not simple conjecture, how can we conceive an absolute extrinsic determination, when the act in birth only makes one with the finished sum of its conditions, when these conditions are complete only on the threshold of the action beginning, including the fresh and irreducible contribution added by its very date in our history? We can only explain afterwards, we can only foresee when it is too late, in retrospect, when the accomplished action has fallen into the plan of matter.

Thus our inner life is a work of enduring creation: of phases which mature slowly, and conclude at long intervals the decisive moments of emancipating discovery. Undoubtedly matter is there, under the forms of habit, threatening us with automatism, seeking at every moment to devour us, stealing a march on us whenever we forget. But matter represents in us only the waste of existence, the mortal fall of weakened reality, the swoon of the creative action falling back inert; while the depths of our being still pulse with the liberty which, in its true function, employs mechanism itself only as a means of action.

Now, does not this conception make a singular exception of us in nature, an empire within an empire? That is the question we have yet to investigate.

II

We have just attempted to grasp what being is in ourselves; and we have found that it is becoming, progress, and growth, that it is a creative process which never ceases to labour incessantly; in a word, that it is duration. Must we come to the same conclusion about external being, about existence in general?

Let us consider that external reality which is nearest us, our body. It is known to us both externally by our perceptions and internally by our affections. It is then a privileged case for our inquiry. In addition, and by analogy, we shall at the same time study the

TEACHING

other living bodies which everyday induction shows us to be more or less like our own. What are the distinctive characteristics of these new realities? Each of them possesses a genuine individuality to a far greater degree than inorganic objects; whilst the latter are hardly limited at all except in relation to the needs of the former, and so do not constitute beings in themselves, the former evidence a powerful internal unity which is only further emphasised by their prodigious complication, and form wholes which are naturally complete. These wholes are not collections of juxtaposed parts: they are organisms; that is to say, systems of connected functions, in which each detail implies the whole, and where the various elements interpenetrate. These organisms change and modify continually; we say of them not only that they *are*, but that they *live*; and their life is mutability itself, a flight, a perpetual flux. This uninterrupted flight cannot in any way be compared to a geometrical movement; it is a rhythmic succession of phases, each of which contains the resonance of all those which come before; each state lives on in the state following; the life of the body is memory; the living being accumulates its past, makes a snowball of itself, serves as an open register for time, ripens, and grows old. Despite all resemblances, the living body always remains, in some measure, an absolutely original and unique invention, for there are not two specimens exactly alike; and, among inert objects, it appears as the reservoir of indetermination, the centre of spontaneity, contingence, and genuine action, as if in the course of phenomena nothing really new could be produced except by its agency.

Such are the characteristic tendencies of life, such the aspects which it presents to immediate observation. Whether spiritual activity unconsciously presides over biological evolution, or whether it simply prolongs it, we always find here and there the essential features of duration.

But I spoke just now of "individuality." Is it really one of the distinctive marks of life? We know how difficult it is to define it accurately. Nowhere, not even in man, is it fully realised; and there are beings in existence in which it seems a complete illusion, though every part of them reproduces their complete unity.

True, but we are now dealing with biology, in which geometrical precision is inadmissible, where reality is defined not so much by the possession of certain characteristics as by its tendency to accentuate them. It is as a tendency that individuality is more particularly manifested; and if we look at it in this light, no one can deny that it does constitute one of the fundamental tendencies of life. Only the truth is that the tendency to individuality remains always and everywhere counterbalanced, and therefore limited, by an opposing tendency, the tendency to association, and above all to reproduction. This necessitates a correction in our analysis. Nature, in many respects, seems to take no interest in individuals. "Life appears to be a current passing from one germ to another through the medium of a developed organism." [1]

It seems as if the organism played the part of a thoroughfare. What is important is rather the continuity of progress of which the individuals are only transitory phases. Between these phases again there are no sharp severances; each phase resolves and melts imperceptibly into that which follows. Is not the real problem of heredity to know how, and up to what point, a new individual breaks away from the individuals which produced it? Is not the real mystery of heredity

[1] *Creative Evolution*, p. 29.

the difference, not the resemblance, occurring between one term and another?

Whatever be its solution, all the individual phases mutually extend and interpenetrate one another. There is a racial memory by which the past is continually accumulated and preserved. Life's history is embodied in its present. And that is really the ultimate reason of the perpetual novelty which surprised us just now. The characteristics of biological evolution are thus the same as those of human progress. Once again we find the very stuff of reality in duration. "We must not then speak any longer of *life in general* as an abstraction, or a mere heading under which we write down all living beings."[1] On the contrary, to it belongs the primordial function of reality. It is a very real current transmitted from generation to generation, organising and passing through bodies, without failing or becoming exhausted in any one of them.

We may already, then, draw one conclusion: *Reality, at bottom, is becoming*. But such a thesis runs counter to all our familiar ideas. It is imperative that we should submit it to the test of critical examination and positive verification.

[1] *Creative Evolution*, p. 28.

One system of metaphysics, I said some time ago, underlies common-sense, animating and informing it. According to this system, which is the inverse of that which we have just intimated, reality in its very depths is fixity and permanence. This is the completely static conception which sees in *being* exactly the opposite of *becoming*: we cannot become, it seems to say, except in so far as we are not. It does not, however, mean to deny movement. But it represents it as fluctuation round invariable types, as a whirling but captive eddy. Every phenomenon appears to it as a transformation which ends where it began, and the result is that the world takes the form of an eternal equilibrium in which " nothing is created, nothing destroyed." The idea does not need much forcing to end in the old supposition of a cyclic return which restores everything to its original conditions. Everything is thus conceived in astronomical periods. All that is left of the universe henceforward is a whirl of atoms in which nothing counts but certain fixed quantities translated by our systems of equations; the rest has vanished " in algebraical smoke." There is therefore nothing more or less in the effect than in the group of causes; and the causal relation moves towards identity as towards its asymptote.

Such a view of nature is open to many objections, even if it were only a question of inorganised matter. Simple physics already betoken the insufficiency of a purely mechanic conception. The stream of phenomena flows in an irreversible direction and obeys a determined rhythm. "If I wish to prepare myself a glass of sugar and water, I may do what I like, but I must wait for my sugar to melt."[1] Here are facts which pure mechanism does not take into account, regarding as it does only statically conceived relations, and making time into a measure only, something like a common denominator of concrete successions, a certain number of coincidences from which all true duration remains absent, which would remain unchanged even if the world's history, instead of opening out in consecutive phases, were to be unfolded before our eyes all at once like a fan. Do we not indeed speak to-day of aging and atomic separation. If the quantity of energy is preserved, at least its quality is continually deteriorating. By the side of something which remains constant, the world also contains something

[1] *Creative Evolution*, p. 10.

which is being used up, dissipated, exhausted, decomposed.

Further still, a specimen of metal, in its molecular structure, preserves an indelible trace of the treatment it has undergone; natural philosophers tell us that there is a "memory of solids." These are all very positive facts which pure mechanism passes over. In addition, must we not first of all postulate what will afterwards be preserved or deteriorated? Whence we get another aspect of things: that of *genesis* and *creation*; and in reality we register the ascending effort of life as a reality no less startling than mechanic inertia.

Finally, we have a double movement of ascent and descent: such is what life and matter appear to immediate observation. These two currents meet each other, and grapple. It is the drama of evolution, of which Mr Bergson once gave a masterly explanation, in stating the high place which man fills in nature:

"I cannot regard the general evolution and progress of life in the whole of the organised world, the co-ordination and subordination of vital functions to one another in the same living being, the relations which psychology and physiology combined seem bound to establish between brain activity and thought in man, without arriving at this conclusion, that life is an immense effort attempted by thought to obtain of matter something which matter does not wish to give it. Matter is inert; it is the seat of necessity; it proceeds mechanically. It seems as if thought seeks to profit by this mechanical inclination in matter to utilise it for *actions*, and thus to convert all the creative energy it contains, at least all that this energy possesses which admits of *play* and external extraction, into contingent movements in space and events in time which cannot be foreseen. With laborious research it piles up complications to make liberty out of necessity, to compose for itself a matter so subtile, and so mobile, that liberty, by a veritable physical paradox, and thanks to an effort which cannot last long, succeeds in maintaining its equilibrium on this very mobility.

" But it is caught in the snare. The eddy on which it was poised seizes and drags it down. It becomes prisoner of the mechanism it has set up. Automatism lays hold of it, and life, inevitably forgetting the end which it had determined, which was only to be a means in view of a superior end, is entirely

TEACHING

used up in an effort to preserve itself by itself. From the humblest of organised beings to the higher vertebrates which come immediately before man, we witness an attempt which is always foiled and always resumed with more and more art. Man has triumphed; with difficulty, it is true, and so incompletely that a moment's lapse and inattention on his part surrender him to automatism again. But he has triumphed. . . ."[1]

And Mr Bergson adds in another place:[2] "With man consciousness breaks the chain. In man and in man only it obtains its freedom. The whole history of life, till man, had been the history of an effort of consciousness to lift matter, and of the more or less complete crushing of consciousness by matter falling upon it again. The enterprise was paradoxical; if indeed we can speak here, except paradoxically, of enterprise and effort. The task was to take matter, which is necessity itself, and create an instrument of liberty, construct a mechanical system to triumph over mechanism, to employ the determinism of nature to pass through the meshes of the

[1] *Report of the French Philosophical Society*, meeting, 2nd May 1901.
[2] *Creative Evolution*, pp. 286–287.

net it had spread. But everywhere, except in man, consciousness let itself be caught in the net of which it sought to traverse the meshes. It remained taken in the mechanisms it had set up. The automatism which it claimed to be drawing towards liberty enfolds it and drags it down. It has not the strength to get away, because the energy with which it had supplied itself for action is almost entirely employed in maintaining the exceedingly subtle and essentially unstable equilibrium into which it has brought matter. But man does not merely keep his machine going, he succeeds in using it as it pleases him.

"He owes it without doubt to the superiority of his brain, which allows him to construct an unlimited number of motor mechanisms, to oppose new habits to old time after time, and to master automatism by dividing it against itself. He owes it to his language, which furnishes consciousness with an immaterial body in which to become incarnate, thus dispensing it from depending exclusively upon material bodies, the flux of which would drag it down and soon engulf it. He owes it to social life, which stores and preserves efforts as language stores thought, thereby fixing a mean level to which individuals will rise with ease, and which, by means of this initial impulse, prevents average individuals from going to sleep and urges better people to rise higher. But our brain, our society, and our language are only the varied outer signs of one and the same internal superiority. Each after its fashion, they tell us the unique and exceptional success which life has won at a given moment of its evolution. They translate the difference in nature, and not in degree only, which separates man from the rest of the animal world. They let us see that if, at the end of the broad springboard from which life took off, all others came down, finding the cord stretched too high, man alone has leapt the obstacle."

But man is not on that account isolated in nature : " As the smallest grain of dust forms part of our entire solar system, and is involved along with it in this undivided downward movement which is materiality itself, so all organised beings from the humblest to the highest, from the first origins of life to the times in which we live, and in all places as at all times, do but demonstrate to our eyes a unique impulse contrary to the movement of matter, and, in itself, indivisible. All living beings are connected, and all yield to the same formidable thrust. The animal is supported by the plant, man rides the animal, and the whole of humanity in space and time is an immense army galloping by the side of each of us, before and behind us, in a spirited charge which can upset all resistance, and leap many obstacles, perhaps even death."[1]

We see with what broad and far-reaching conclusions the new philosophy closes. In the forcible poetry of the pages just quoted its original accent rings deep and pure. Some of its leading theses, moreover, are noted here. But now we must discover the solid foundation of underlying fact.

Let us take first the fact of biological evolution. Why has it been selected as the basis of the system? Is it really a fact, or is it only a more or less conjectural and plausible theory?

Notice in the first instance that the argument from evolution appears at least as a weapon of co-ordination and research admitted in our day by all philosophers, rejected only on the inspiration of preconceived ideas which are completely unscientific; and that it succeeds in the task allotted to it is doubtless already the proof that it responds to some part of reality. And besides, we can go further.

[1] *Creative Evolution*, pp. 293-294.

"The idea of transformism is already contained in germ in the natural classification of organised beings. The naturalist brings resembling organisms together, divides the group into sub-groups, within which the resemblance is still greater, and so on; throughout the operation, the characteristics of the group appear as general themes upon which each of the sub-groups executes its particular variations.

"Now this is precisely the relation we find in the animal world and in the vegetable world between that which produces and what is produced; on the canvas bequeathed by the ancestor to his posterity, and possessed in common by them, each broiders his original pattern."[1]

We may, it is true, ask ourselves whether the genealogical method permits results so far divergent as those presented to us by variety of species. But embryology answers by showing us the highest and most complex forms of life attained every day from very elementary forms; and palæontology, as it develops, allows us to witness the same spectacle in the universal history of life, as if the succession of phases through which the embryo passes were

[1] *Creative Evolution*, pp. 24–25.

only a recollection and an epitome of the complete past whence it has come. In addition, the phenomena of sudden changes, recently observed, help us to understand more easily the conception which obtrudes itself under so many heads, by diminishing the importance of the apparent lacunæ in genealogical continuity. Thus the trend of all our experience is the same.

Now there are some certainties which are only centres of concurrent probabilities; there are some truths determined only by succession of facts, but yet, by their intersection and convergence, sufficiently determined.

"That is how we measure the distance from an inaccessible point, by regarding it time after time from the points to which we have access."[1]

Is not that the case here? The affirmative seems all the more inevitable inasmuch as the language of transformism is the only language known to the biology of to-day. Evolution can, it is true, be transposed, but not suppressed, since in any actual state there would always remain this striking fact that the living forms met with as remains in geological layers are

[1] *Report of the French Philosophical Society*, meeting, 2nd May 1901.

ranged by the natural affinity of their characteristics in an order of succession parallel to the succession of the ages. We are not really then inventing a hypothesis in beginning with the affirmation of evolution. But what we have to do is to appreciate its object.

Evolution! We meet the word everywhere to-day. But how rare is the true idea! Let us ask the astronomers who originate cosmogonical hypotheses, and invent a primitive nebula, the natural philosophers who dream that by the deterioration of energy and the dissipation of movement the material world will obtain final rest in the inertia of a homogeneous equilibrium; let us ask the biologists and psychologists who are enemies of fixed species and inquisitive about ancestral history. What they are anxious to discern in evolution is the persistent influence of an initial cause once given, the attraction of a fixed end, a collection of laws before the eternity of which change becomes negligible like an appearance. Now he who thinks of the universe as a construction of unchangeable relations denies by his method the evolution of which he speaks, since he transforms it into a calculable effect necessarily produced by a regulated play of generating conditions, since he implicitly admits the illusive character of a becoming which adds nothing to what is given.

Finality itself, if he keeps the name, does not save him from his error, for finality in his eyes is nothing but an efficient cause projected into the future. So we see him fixing stages, marking periods, inserting means, putting in milestones, continually destroying movement by halting it before his gaze. And we all do the same by instinctive inclination. Our concept of law, in its classical form, is not general: it represents only the law of co-existence and of mechanism, the static relation between two numerically disconnected terms; and in order to grasp evolution we shall doubtless have to invent a new type of law: law in duration, dynamic relation. For we can, and we must, conceive that there is an evolution of natural laws; that these laws never define anything but a momentary state of things; that they are in reality like streaks determined in the flux of becoming by the meeting of contrary currents. "Laws," says Monsieur Boutroux, "are the bed down which passes the torrent of facts; they have dug it, though they follow it." Yet we see the common theories of evolution appealing to the concepts of the present to describe the past, forcing them back to prehistoric times, and beyond the reasoning of to-day, placing at the beginning what is only conceivable in the mind of the contemporary thinker; in a word, imagining the same laws as always existing and always observed. This is the method which Mr Bergson so justly criticises in Spencer: that of reconstructing evolution with fragments of its product.

If we wish thoroughly to grasp the reality of things, we must think otherwise. Neither of these ready-made concepts, mechanism and finality, is in place, because both of them imply the same postulate, viz. that "everything is given," either at the beginning or at the end, whilst evolution is nothing if it is not, on the contrary, "that which gives." Let us take care not to confound evolution and development. There is the stumbling-block of the usual transformist theories, and Mr Bergson devotes to it a closely argued and singularly penetrating criticism, by an example which he analyses in detail.[1] These theories either do not explain the birth of variation, and limit themselves to an attempt to make us understand how, once born, it becomes fixed, or else through need of adaptation they look for a

[1] *Creative Evolution*, chap. i.

conception of its birth. But in both cases they fail.

" The truth is that adaptation explains the windings of the movement of evolution, but not the general directions of the movement, still less the movement itself. The road which leads to the town is certainly obliged to climb the hills and go down the slopes; it adapts itself to the accidents of the ground ; but the accidents of the ground are not the cause of the road, any more than they have imparted its direction."[1]

At the bottom of all these errors there are only prejudices of practical action. That is of course why every work appears to be an outside construction beginning with previous elements; a phase of anticipation followed by a phase of execution, calculation, and art, an effective projecting cause, and a concerted goal, a mechanism which hurls to a finality which aims. But the genuine explanation must be sought elsewhere. And Mr Bergson makes this plain by two admirable analyses in which he takes to pieces the common ideas of *disorder* and *nothingness* in order to explain their meaning relative to our proceedings in industry or language.

[1] *Creative Evolution*, pp. 111-112.

Let us come back to facts, to immediate experience, and try to translate its pure data simply. What are the characteristics of vital evolution? First of all it is a dynamic continuity, a continuity of qualitative progress; next, it is essentially a duration, an irreversible rhythm, a work of inner maturation. By the memory inherent in it, the whole of its past lives on and accumulates, the whole of its past remains for ever present to it; which is tantamount to saying that it is experience.

It is also an effort of perpetual invention, a generation of continual novelty, inedicible and capable of defying all anticipation, as it defies all repetition. We see it at its task of research in the groping attempts exhibited by the long-sought genesis of species; we see it triumphant in the originality of the least state of consciousness, of the least body, of the tiniest cell, of which the infinity of times and spaces does not offer two identical specimens.

But the reef which lies in its way, and on which too often it founders, is habit; habit would be a better and more powerful means of action if it remained free, but in so far as it congeals and becomes materialised, is a hindrance and an obstacle. First of all we have the average types round which fluctuates an action which is decreasing and becoming reduced in breadth. Then we have the residual organs, the proofs of dead life, the encrustations from which the stream of consciousness gradually ebbs; and finally we have the inert gear from which all real life has disappeared, the masses of shipwrecked "things" rearing their spectral outlines where once rolled the open sea of mind. The concept of mechanism suits the phenomena which occur within the zone of wreckage, on this shore of fixities and corpses. But life itself is rather finality, if not in the anthropomorphic sense of premeditated design, plan, or programme, at least in this sense, that it is a continually renewed effort of growth and liberation. And it is from here we get Mr Bergson's formulæ: vital impetus and creative evolution.

In this conception of being consciousness is everywhere, as original and fundamental reality, always present in a myriad degrees of tension or sleep, and under infinitely various rhythms.

The vital impulse consists in a "demand for creation"; life in its humblest stage already constitutes a spiritual activity; and its effort sends out a current of ascending realisation which again determines the counter-current of matter. Thus all reality is contained in a double movement of ascent and descent. The first only, which translates an inner work of creative maturation, is essentially *durable*; the second might, in strictness, be almost instantaneous, like that of an escaping spring; but the one imposes its rhythm on the other. From this point of view mind and matter appear not as two *things* opposed to each other, as static terms in fixed antithesis, but rather as two inverse directions of movement; and, in certain respects, we must therefore speak not so much of matter or mind as of *spiritualisation* and *materialisation*, the latter resulting automatically from a simple interruption of the former. " Consciousness or superconsciousness is the rocket, the extinguished remains of which fall into matter."[1]

What image of universal evolution is then suggested? Not a cascade of deduction, nor a system of stationary pulsations, but a fountain which spreads like a sheaf of corn and is partially arrested, or at least hindered and delayed, by the falling spray. The fountain itself, the reality which is created, is vital activity, of which spiritual activity represents the highest form; and the spray which falls

[1] *Creative Evolution*, p. 283.

is the creative act which falls, it is reality which is undone, it is matter and inertia. In a word, the supreme law of genesis and fall, the double play of which constitutes the universe, comprises a psychological formula.

Everything begins in the manner of an invention, as the fruit of duration and creative genius, by liberty, by pure mind; then comes habit, a kind of body, as the body is already a group of habits; and habit, taking root, being a work of consciousness which escapes it and turns against it, is little by little degraded into mechanism in which the soul is buried.

III

The main lines and general perspective of Mr Bergson's philosophy now perhaps begin to appear. Certainly I am the first to feel how powerless a slender résumé really is to translate all its wealth and all its strength.

At least I wish I could have contributed to making its movement, and what I may call its rhythm, clearer to perception. It is from the books of the master himself that a more complete revelation must be sought. And the few words which I am still going to add as conclusion are only intended to sketch the principal consequences of the doctrine, and allow its distant reach to be seen.

The evolution of life would be a very simple and easy thing to understand if it were fulfilled along one single trajectory and followed a straight path. " But we are here dealing with a shell which has immediately burst into fragments, which, being themselves species of shells, have again burst into fragments destined to burst again, and so on for a very long time."[1] It is, in fact, the property of a tendency to develop itself in the expansion which analyses it. As for the causes of this dispersion into kingdoms, then into species, and finally into individuals, we can distinguish two series: the resistance which matter opposes to the current of life sent through it, and the explosive force—due to an unstable equilibrium of tendencies—carried by the vital impulse within itself. Both unite in making the thrust of life divide in more and more diverging but complementary directions, each emphasising some distinct aspect of its original wealth. Mr Bergson confines himself to the branches of the first order—plant, animal, and man. And in the course of a minute and searching discussion he shows us the character-

[1] *Creative Evolution*, p. 107.

istics of these lines in the moods or qualities signified by the three words—*torpor, instinct,* and *intelligence*: the vegetable kingdom constructing and storing explosives which the animal expends, and man creating a nervous system for himself which permits him to convert the expense into analysis. Let us leave aside, as we must, the many suggestive views scattered lavishly about, the many flashes of light which fall on all faces of the problem, and let us confine ourselves to seeing how we get a theory of knowledge from this doctrine. There we have yet another proof of the striking and fertile originality of the new philosophy.

More than one objection has been brought against Mr Bergson on this head. That is quite natural: how could such a novelty be exactly understood at once? It is also very desirable; it is the demands for enlightenment which lead a doctrine to full consciousness of itself, to precision and perfection. But we must be afraid of false objections, those which arise from an obstinate translation of the new philosophy into an old language steeped in a different metaphysic. With what has Mr Bergson been reproached? With misunderstanding reason, with ruining positive science, with being caught in the illusion of getting knowledge otherwise than by intelligence, or of thinking otherwise than by thought; in short, of falling into a vicious circle by making intellectualism turn round upon itself. Not one of these reproaches has any foundation.

Let us begin by a few preliminary remarks to clear the ground. First of all, there is one ridiculous objection which I quote only to record. I mean that which suspects at the bottom of the theories which we are going to discuss some dark background, some prepossession of irrational mysticism. On the contrary, the truth is, we have here perhaps better than anywhere, the spectacle of pure thought face to face with things. But it is a complete thought, not thought reduced to some partial functions, but sufficiently sure of its critical power to sacrifice none of its resources. Here, we may say, really is the genuine positivism, which reinstates all spiritual reality. It does not in any way lead to a misunderstanding or depreciation of science. Even where contingency and relativity are most visible in it, in the domain of inert matter, Mr Bergson goes so far as to say that physical science touches an absolute. It is true that it *touches* this absolute rather than *sees* it. More particularly it perceives all its reactions on a system of representative forms which it presents to it, and observes the effect on the veil of theory with which it envelops it. At certain moments, all the same, the veil becomes almost transparent. And in any case the scholar's thought guesses and grazes reality in the curve drawn by the succession of its increasing syntheses. But there are two orders of science. Formerly it was from the mathematician that we borrowed the ideal of evidence. Hence came the inclination always to seek the most certain knowledge from the most abstract side. The temptation was to make a kind of less severe and rigorous mathematics of biology itself. Now if such a method suits the study of inert matter because in a manner geometrical, so much so that our knowledge of it thus acquired is more incomplete than inexact, this is not at all the case for the things of life. Here, if we were to conduct scientific research always in the same grooves and according to the same formulæ, we should immediately encounter symbolism and relativity. For life is *progress*, whilst the geometrical method is commensurable only with *things*. Mr Bergson is aware of this; and his rare merit has been to disengage specific originality from biology, while elevating it to a typical and standard science.

But let us come to the heart of the problem. What was Kant's point of departure in the theory of knowledge? In seeking to define the structure of the mind according to the traces of itself which it must have left in its works, and in proceeding by a reflective analysis ascending from a fact to its conditions, he could only regard intelligence as a thing made, a fixed system of categories and principles.

Mr Bergson adopts an inverse attitude. Intelligence is a product of evolution : we see it slowly and uninterruptedly constructed along a line which rises through the vertebrates to man. Such a point of view is the only one which conforms to the real nature of things, and the actual conditions of reality ; the more we think of it, the more we perceive that the *theory of knowledge* and the *theory of life* are bound up with one another. Now what do we conclude from this point of view? Life, considered in the direction of "knowledge," evolves on two diverging lines which at first are confused, then gradually separate, and finally end in two opposed forms of organisation, intelligence and instinct. Several contrary potentialities interpenetrated at their common source, but of this source each of these kinds of activity preserves or rather accentuates only one tendency; and it will be easy to mark its dual character.

Instinct is sympathy; it has no clear consciousness of itself; it does not know how to reflect; it is hardly capable of varying its steps; but it operates with incomparable certainty because it remains lodged in things, in communion with their rhythm and with inner feeling of them. The history of animals in this respect supplies many remarkable examples which Mr Bergson analyses and discusses in detail. As much might be said of the work which produces a living body, and of the effort which presides over its growth, maintenance, and functions. Take a natural philosopher who has long breathed the atmosphere of the laboratory, who has by long practice acquired what we call "experience"; he has a kind of intimate feeling for his instruments, their resources, their movements, their working tendencies; he perceives them as extensions of himself; he possesses them as groups of habitual actions, thus discoursing by manipulations as easily and spontaneously as others discourse in calculation. Doubtless that is only an image;

but transpose it and generalise it, and it will help you to understand the kind of action which divines instinct. But intelligence is something quite different. We are talking, of course, of the analytic and synthetic intelligence which we use in our acts of current thought, which works throughout our daily action and forms the fundamental thread of our scientific operations. I need not here go back to the criticism of its ordinary proceedings. But I must now note the service which suits them, the domain in which they apply and are valid, and what they teach us thereby about the meaning, reach, and natural task of intelligence.

Whilst instinct vibrates in sympathetic harmony with life, it is about inert matter that intelligence is granted; it is a rider to our faculty of action; it triumphs in geometry; it feels at home among the objects in which our industry finds its supports and its tools. In a word, "our logic is primarily the logic of solids."[1] But if we enter the vital order its incompetence is manifestly apparent.

It is very significant that deduction should be so impotent in biology. Still more impotent is it perhaps in matters of art or

[1] Preface to *Creative Evolution*.

religion; whilst, on the contrary, it works marvels so long as it has only to foresee movements or transformations in bodies. What does this mean, if not that intelligence and materiality go together, that language with its analytic steps is regulated by the movements of matter? Philosophy once again then must leave it behind, for the duty of philosophy is to consider everything in its relation to life.

Do not conclude, however, that the philosopher's duty is to renounce intelligence, place it under tutelage, or abandon it to the blind suggestions of feeling and will. It has not even the right to do so. Instinct, with us who have evolved along the grooves of intelligence, has remained too weak to be sufficient for us. Besides, intelligence is the only path by which light could dawn in the bosom of primitive darkness. But let us look at present reality in all its complexity, all its wealth. Round intelligence itself exists a halo of instinct. This halo represents the remains of the first nebulous vapour at the expense of which intelligence was constituted like a brilliantly condensed nucleus; and it is still to-day the atmosphere which gives it life, the fringe of touch, and delicate probing, inspiring contact and divining sympathy, which we see in play in the phenomena of discovery, as also in the acts of that "attention to life," and that "sense of reality" which is the soul of *good sense*, so widely distinct from *common-sense*. And the peculiar task of the philosopher is to reabsorb intelligence in instinct, or rather to reinstate instinct in intelligence; or better still, to win back to the heart of intelligence all the initial resources which it must have sacrificed. This is what is meant by return to the primitive, and the immediate, to reality and life. This is the meaning of intuition.

Certainly the task is difficult. We at once suspect a vicious circle. How can we go beyond intelligence except by intelligence itself? We are apparently inside our thought, as incapable of coming out of it as is a balloon of rising above the atmosphere. True, but on this reasoning we could just as well prove that it is impossible for us to acquire any new habit whatsoever, impossible for life to grow and go beyond itself continually.

We must avoid drawing false conclusions from the simile of the balloon. The question here is to know what are the real limits of the atmosphere. It is certain that the synthetic and critical intelligence, left to its own strength, remains imprisoned in a circle from which there is no escape.

But action removes the barrier. If intelligence accepts the risk of taking the leap into the phosphorescent fluid which bathes it, and to which it is not altogether foreign, since it has broken off from it and in it dwell the complementary powers of the understanding, intelligence will soon become adapted and so will only be lost for a moment to reappear greater, stronger, and of fuller content. It is action again under the name of experience which removes the danger of illusion or giddiness, it is action which *verifies*; by a practical demonstration, by an effort of enduring maturation which tests the idea in intimate contact with reality and judges it by its fruits.

It always falls therefore to intelligence to pronounce the grand verdict in the sense that only that can be called true which will finally satisfy it; but we mean an intelligence duly enlarged and transformed by the very effect of the action it has lived. Thus the objection of "irrationalism" directed against the new philosophy falls to the ground.

The objection of "non-morality" fares no better. But it has been made, and people have thought fit to accuse Mr Bergson's work of being the too calm production of an intelligence too indifferent, too coldly lucid, too exclusively curious to see and understand, untroubled and unthrilled by the universal drama of life, by the tragic reality of evil. On the other hand, not without contradiction, the new philosophy has been called "romantic," and people have tried to find in it the essential traits of romanticism: its predilection for feeling and imagination, its unique anxiety for vital intensity, its recognised right to all which is to be, whence its radical inability to establish a hierarchy of moral qualifications. Strange reproach! The system in question is not yet presented to us as a finished system. Its author manifests a plain desire to classify his problems. And he is certainly right in proceeding so: there is a time for everything, and on occasion we must learn to be just an eye focussed upon being. But that does not at all exclude the possibility of future works, treating in due order of the problem of human destiny, and perhaps even in the work so far completed we may descry some attempts to bring this future within ken.

But universal evolution, though creative, is not for all that quixotic or anarchist. It forms a sequence. It is a becoming with direction, undoubtedly due, not to the attraction of a clearly preconceived goal, or the guidance of an outer law, but to the actual tendency of the original thrust. In spite of the stationary eddies or momentary backwashes we observe here and there, its stream moves in a definite direction, ever swelling and broadening. For the spectator who regards the general sweep of the current, evolution is growth. On the other hand, he who thinks this growth now ended is under a simple delusion: "The gates of the future stand wide open."[1] In the stage at present attained man is leading; he marks the culminating point at which creation continues; in him, life has already succeeded, at least up to a certain point; from him onwards it advances with consciousness capable of reflection; is it not for that very reason responsible for the result? Life, according to the new philosophy, is a continual creation of what is new: new—be it well understood—in the sense of growth and progress in relation to what has gone before. Life, in a word, is mental travel, ascent in a path of growing spiritualisation. Such at least is the intense desire, and such the first tendency which

[1] *Creative Evolution*, p. 114.

launched and still inspires it. But it may faint, halt, or travel down the hill. This is an undeniable fact; and once recognised does it not awake in us the presentiment of a directing law immanent in vital effort, a law doubtless not to be found in any code, nor yet binding through the stern behest of mechanical necessity, but a law which finds definition at every moment, and at every moment also marks a direction of progress, being as it were the shifting tangent to the curve of becoming?

Let us add that according to the new philosophy the whole of our past survives for ever in us, and by means of us results in action. It is then literally true that our acts do to a certain extent involve the whole universe, and its whole history: the act which we make it accomplish will exist henceforward for ever, and will for ever tinge universal duration with its indelible shade. Does not that imply an imperious, urgent, solemn, and tragic problem of action? Nay, more; memory makes a persistent reality of evil, as of good. Where are we to find the means to abolish and reabsorb the evil? What in the individual is called memory becomes tradition and joint responsibility in the race.

On the other hand, a directing law is immanent in life, but in the shape of an appeal to endless transcendence. In dealing with this future transcendent to our daily life, with this further shore of present experience, where are we to seek the inspiring strength? And is there not ground for asking ourselves whether intuitions have not arisen here and there in the course of history, lighting up the dark road of the future for us with a prophetic ray of dawn? It is at this point that the new philosophy would find place for the problem of religion.

But this word "religion," which has not come once so far from Mr Bergson's pen, coming now from mine, warns me that it is time to end. No man to-day would be justified in foreseeing the conclusions to which the doctrine of creative évolution will one day undoubtedly lead on this point. More than any other, I must forget here what I myself may have elsewhere tried to do in this order of ideas. But it was impossible not to feel the approach of the temptation. Mr Bergson's work is extraordinarily suggestive. His books, so measured in tone, so tranquil in harmony, awaken in us a mystery of presentiment and imagination; they reach the hidden retreats where the springs of consciousness well up. Long after we have closed them we are shaken within; strangely moved, we listen to the deepening echo, passing on and on. However valuable already their explicit contents may be, they reach still further than they aimed. It is impossible to tell what latent germs they foster. It is impossible to guess what lies behind the boundless distance of the horizons they expose. But this at least is sure: these books have verily begun a new work in the history of human thought.

ADDITIONAL EXPLANATIONS

I

MR BERGSON'S WORK AND THE GENERAL DIRECTIONS OF CONTEMPORARY THOUGHT

A BROAD survey of the new philosophy was bound to be somewhat rapid and summary; and now that this is completed it will doubtless not be superfluous to come back, on the same plan as before, to some more important or more difficult individual points, and to examine by themselves the most prominent centres on which we should focus the light of our attention. Not that I intend to probe in minute detail the folds and turns of a doctrine which admits of infinite development: how can I claim to exhaust a work of such profound thought that the least passing example employed takes its place as a particular study? Still less do I wish to undertake a kind of analytic résumé; no undertaking could be less profitable than that of arranging paragraph headings to repeat too briefly, and therefore obscurely, what a thinker has said without any extravagance of language, yet with every requisite explanation.

The critic's true task, as I understand it, in no way consists in drawing up a table of contents strewn with qualifying notes. His task is to read and enable others to read between the lines, between the chapters, and between the successive works, what constitutes the dynamic tie between them, all that the linear form of writing and language has not allowed the author himself to elucidate.

His task is, as far as possible, to master the accompaniment of underlying thought which produced the resonant atmosphere of the inquirer's intuition, the rhythm and toning of the image, resulting in the shade of light which falls upon his vision. His task, in a word, is to help understanding, and therefore to point out and anticipate the misunderstandings to be feared. Now it seems to me that there are a few points round which the errors of interpretation more naturally gather, producing some astounding misconceptions of Mr Bergson's philosophy. It is these points only that I propose to clear up. But at the same time I shall use the opportunity to supply information about authorities, which I have hitherto deliberately omitted, to avoid riddling with references pages which were primarily intended to impart a general impression.

Let us begin by glancing at the *milieu* of thought in which Mr Bergson's philosophy must have had birth. For the last thirty years new currents are traceable. In what direction do they go? And what distance have they already gone? What, in short, are the intellectual characteristics of our time? We must endeavour to distinguish the deeper tendencies, those which herald and prepare the near future.

One of the essential and frequently cited features of the generation in which Taine and Renan were the most prominent leaders was the passionate, enthusiastic, somewhat exclusive and intolerant cult of positive science. This science, in its days of pride, was considered unique, displayed on a plane by itself, always uniformly competent, capable of gripping any object whatever with the same strength, and of inserting it in the thread of one and the same unbroken connection.

The dream of that time, despite all verbal palliations, was a universal science of mathematics: mathematics, of course, with their bare and brutal rigour softened and shaded off, where feasible; if possible, supple and sensitive; in ideal, delicate, buoyant, and judicious; but mathematics governed from end to end by an equal necessity. Conceived as the sole mistress of truth, this science was expected in days to come to fulfil all the needs of man, and unreservedly to take the place of ancient spiritual discipline. Genuine philosophy had had its day: all metaphysics seemed deception and fantasy, a simple play of empty formulæ or puerile dreams, a mythical procession of abstraction and phantom; religion itself paled before science, as poetry of the grey morning before the splendour of the rising sun.

However, after all this pride came the turn of humility, and humility of the very lowest. This deified science, borne down in its hour of triumph by too heavy a weight, had necessarily been recognised as powerless to go beyond the order of relations, and radically incapable of telling us the origin, end, and basis of things. It analysed the conditions of phenomena, but was ill-suited ever to grasp any real cause, or any deep essence. Further, it became the Unknowable, before which the human mind could only halt in despair. And in this way destitution arose out of ambition itself, since thought, after trusting too exclusively to its geometrical strength, was compelled at the end of its effort to confess itself beaten when confronted with the only questions to which no man may ever be indifferent.

This double attitude is no longer that of the contemporary generation. The prestige of illusion has vanished. In the religion of science we see now nothing but idolatry. The haughty affirmation of yesterday appears today, not as expressing a positive fact or a result duly established, but as bringing forward a thesis of perilous and unconscious metaphysics. Let us go even further. If true intelligence is mental expansion and aptitude for understanding widely different things, each in its originality, to the same degree, we must say that the claim to reduce reality to one only of its modes, to know it in one only of its forms, is an unintelligent claim. That is, in brief formula, the verdict of the present generation. Not, of course, that it in any way misconceives or disdains the true value of science, whether as an instrument of action for the conquest of nature, or as intelligible language, allowing us to know our whereabouts in things and " talk " them.

It is aware that in all circumstances positive methods have their evidence to produce, and that, where they pronounce within the limits of their power, nothing can stand against their verdict. But it considers first of all that science was conceived of late under much too stiff and narrow a form, under the obsession of too abstract a mathematical ideal which corresponds to one aspect of reality only, and that the shallowest. And it considers afterwards that science, even when broadened and made flexible, being concerned only with what is, with fact and datum, remains radically powerless to solve the problem of human life. Nowhere does science penetrate to the very depth of things, and there is nothing in the world but " things."

Experience has shown where the dream of universal mathematics leads us. Number is driven to the heart of phenomena and nature dissected with this delicate scalpel. Speaking in more general terms, we adopt spatial relation as the perfect example of intelligible relation. I do not wish to deny the use of such a method now and again, the services it may render, or the beauty of construction peculiar to the systems it inspires. But we must see what price we pay for these advantages. Do we choose geometry for an informing and regulating science? The more we advance towards the concrete and the living, the more we feel the necessity of altering the pure mathematical type. The sciences, as they get further from inert matter, unless they agree to reform, pale and weaken; they become vague, impotent, anæmic; they touch little but the trite surface of their object, the body, not the soul; in them symbolism, artifice, and relativity become increasingly evident; at length, arbitrary and conventional elements crop up and devour them. In a word, the claim to treat the living as inert matter conduces to the misconception in life of life itself, and the retention of nothing but the material waste.

This experience furnishes us with a lesson. There is not so much one science as several sciences, each distinguished by an autonomous method, and divided into two great kingdoms.

Let us therefore from the outset follow Mr Bergson in tracing a very sharp line of demarcation between the inert and the living. Two orders of knowledge will thereby become separate, one in which the frames of geometrical understanding are in place, the other where new means and a new attitude are required. The essential task of the present hour will now appear to us in a precise light; it will henceforward consist, without any disregard of a glorious past, in an effort to found as specifically distinct methods of instruction those sciences which take for objects the successive moments of life in its different degrees, biology, psychology, sociology;—then in an effort to reconstruct, setting out from these new sciences and according to their spirit, the like of what ancient philosophy had attempted, setting out from geometry and mechanics. By so doing we shall succeed in throwing knowledge open to receive all the wealth of reality, while at the same time we shall reinstate the sense of mystery and the thrill of higher anxieties. A further result will be that the phantom of the Unknowable will be exorcised, since it no longer represents anything but the relative and momentary limit of each method, the portion of being which escapes its partial grip.

This is one of the first controlling ideas of the contemporary generation. Others result from it. More particularly, it is for the same body of motives, in the same sense, and with the same restrictions, that we distrust *intellectualism*; I mean the tendency to live uniquely by intelligence, to think as if the whole of thought consisted in analytic, clear and reasoning understanding.

Once again, it is not a question of some blind abandonment to sentiment, imagination, or will, nor do we claim to restrict the legitimate rights of intellectuality in judgment. But around critical reason there is a quickening atmosphere in which dwell the powers of intuition, there is a half-light of gradual tones in which insertion into reality is effected. If by *rationalism* we mean the attitude which consists in cabining ourselves within the zone of geometrical light in which language evolves, we must admit that rationalism supposes something other than itself, that it hangs suspended by a generating act which escapes it.

The method therefore which we seek to employ everywhere to-day is *experience*; but *complete* experience, anxious to neglect no aspect of being nor any resource of mind; *shaded* experience, not extending on the surface only, in a homogeneous and uniform manner; on the contrary, an experience distributed in depth over multiple planes, adopting a thousand different forms to adapt itself to the different kinds of problems; in short, a *creative* and *informing* experience, a veritable genesis, a genuine action of thought, a work and movement of life by which the guiding principles, forms of intelligibility, and criteria of verification obtain birth and stability in habits. And here again it is by borrowing Mr Bergson's own formula from him that we shall most accurately describe the new spirit.

That the attitude and fundamental procedure of this new spirit are in no way a return to scepticism or a reaction against thought cannot be better demonstrated than by this resurrection of metaphysics, this renaissance of idealism, which is certainly one of the most distinctive features of our epoch. Undoubtedly philosophy in France has never known so prosperous and so pregnant a moment. Notwithstanding, it is not a return to the old dreams of dialectic construction. Everything is regarded from the point of view of life, and there is a tendency more and more to recognise the primacy of spiritual activity. But we wish to understand and employ this activity and this life in all its wealth, in all its degrees, and by all its functions: we wish to think with the whole of thought, and go to the truth with the whole of our soul; and the reason of which we recognise the sovereign weight is reason laden with its complete past history.

And what is that, really, but *realism*? By realism I mean the gift of ourselves to reality, the work of concrete realisation, the effort to convert every idea into action, to regulate the idea by the action as much as the action by the idea, to live what we think and think what we live. But that is positivism, you will say; certainly it is positivism. But how changed! Far from considering as positive only that which can be an object of sensation or calculation, we begin by greeting the great spiritual realities with this title. The deep and living aspiration of our day is in everything to seek the soul, the soul which specifies and quickens, seek it by an effort towards the revealing sympathy which is genuine intelligence, seek it in the concrete, without dissolving thought in dreams or language, without losing contact with the body or critical control, seek it, in fine, as the most real and genuine part of being.

Hence its return to questions which were

lately declared out of date and closed; hence its taste for problems of æsthetics and morality, its close siege of social and religious problems, its homesickness for a faith harmonising the powers of action and the powers of thought; hence its restless desire to hark back to tradition and discipline.

A new philosophy was required to answer this new way of looking at things. Already, in 1867, Ravaisson in his celebrated *Report* wrote these prophetic lines: "Many signs permit us to foresee in the near future a philosophical epoch of which the general character will be the predominance of what may be called spiritualist realism or positivism, having as generating principle the consciousness which the mind has in itself of an existence recognised as being the source and support of every other existence, being none other than its action."

This prophetic view was further commented on in a work where Mr Bergson speaks with just praise of this shrewd and penetrating sense of what was coming: "What could be bolder or more novel than to come and predict to the physicists that the inert will be explained by the living, to biologists that life will only be understood by thought, to

138 A NEW PHILOSOPHY

philosophers that generalities are not philosophic?"[1]

But let us give each his due. What Ravaisson had only anticipated Mr Bergson himself accomplishes, with a precision which gives body to the impalpable and floating breath of first inspiration, with a depth which renews both proof and theses alike, with a creative originality which prevents the critic who is anxious for justice and precision from insisting on any researches establishing connection of thought.

One reason for the popularity to-day enjoyed by this new philosophy is doubtless to be found in the very tendencies of the *milieu* in which it is produced and in the aspirations which work it. But, after once remarking these desires, we must further not forget that Mr Bergson has contributed more than anyone else to awaken them, determine them, and make them become conscious of themselves. Let us therefore try to understand in itself and by itself the work of genius of which just now we were seeking the dawning gleams. What synthetic formula will be best able to

[1] *Notice on the Life and Works of M. Félix Ravaisson-Molien*, in the Reports of the Academy of Moral and Political Sciences, 1904.

tell us the essential direction of its movement? I will borrow it from the author himself: " It seems to me," he writes,[1] "that metaphysics are trying at this moment to simplify themselves, to come nearer to life." Every philosophy tends to become incarnate in a system which constitutes for it a kind of body of analysis.

Regarded literally, it appears to be an infinite complication, a complex construction with a thousand alcoves of high architecture, "in which measures have been taken to provide ample lodging for all problems."[2] Do not let us be deceived by this appearance: it signifies only that language is incommensurable with thought, that speech admits of endless multiplication in approximations incapable of exhausting their object. But before constructing such a body for itself, all philosophy is a soul, a mind, and begins with the simple unity of a generating intuition. Here is the fitting point at which to see its essence; this is what determines it much better than its conceptual expression, which is always contingent and incomplete. "A philosophy worthy of the

[1] *Philosophic Intuition* in the *Revue de Métaphysique et de Morale*, November 1911.
[2] *Ibid.*

name has never said but one thing; and that thing it has rather attempted to say than actually said. And it has only said one thing, because it has only seen one point: and that was not so much vision as contact; this contact supplied an impulse, this impulse a movement, and if this movement, which is a kind of vortex of a certain particular form, is only visible to our eyes by what it has picked up on its path, it is no less true that other dust might equally well have been raised, and that it would still have been the same vortex."[1]

Hence comes the fact that a philosophy is at bottom much more independent of its natal environment than one might at first suppose; hence also the fact that ancient philosophies, though apparently relative to a science which is out of date, remain always living and worthy of study.

What, then, is the original intuition of Mr Bergson's philosophy, the creative intuition whence it comes forth? We cannot hesitate long: *it is the intuition of duration*. That is the perspective centre to which we must indefatigably return; that is the principle which we must labour to expose in its full light; and

[1] *Philosophic Intuition* in the *Revue de Métaphysique et de Morale,* November 1911.

that is, finally, the source of light which will illumine us. Now a philosophy is not only an expressed intuition; it is further and above all an acting intuition, gradually determined and realised, and tested by its explanatory works; and it is by its fruits that we can understand and judge it. Hence the review upon which we are entering.

II
IMMEDIACY

THE philosopher's first duty is in clear language to declare his starting-point, with what a mathematician would call the "tangent to the origin" of the path along which he is travelling, as afterwards the critic's first duty is to describe this initial attitude. I have therefore first of all to indicate the directing idea of the new philosophy. But it is not a question of extracting a quintessence, or of fencing the soul of doctrine within a few summary formulæ. A system is not to be resumed in a phrase, for every proposition isolated is a proposition falsified. I wish merely to elucidate the methodical principle which inspires the beginning of Mr Bergson's philosophy.

To philosophy itself falls the task and belongs the right to define itself gradually as it becomes constituted. On this point, an anticipation of experience seems hardly possible; here, as elsewhere, the finding of a synthetic formula is a final rather than preliminary question. However, we are obliged from the outset of the work to determine the programme of the inquiry, if only to direct our research. It is the same on the threshold of every science. There, it is true, the analogy ceases. For in any science properly speaking the determination of beginning consists in the indication of an object, and a matter, and beyond that, to each new object a new science reciprocally corresponds, the existence of the one involving the legitimacy of the other. But if the various sciences—I mean the positive sciences—divide different objects thus between them, philosophy cannot, in its turn, come forward as a particular science, having a distinct object, the designation of which would be sufficient to characterise and circumscribe it. Such was always the traditional conception: such will ours continue to be. For, as a matter of fact, every object has a philosophy and all matter can be regarded philosophically. In short, philosophy is chiefly a way of perceiving and thinking, an attitude and a proceeding: the peculiar and specific in it is more an intuition than a content, a spirit rather than a domain.

What, then, is the characteristic function of philosophy, at least its initial function, that which marks its opening?

To criticise the works of knowledge spontaneously effected; that is to say, to scrutinise their direction, reach, and conditions: that is to-day the unanimous answer of philosophers when questioned about the goal of their labours. In other terms, what they study is not so much such and such a particular "thing" as the relation of mind to each of the realities to be studied. Their object, if we must employ the word, is knowledge itself, it is the act of knowing regarded from the point of view of its meaning and value. Philosophy thus appears as a new "order" of knowledge, co-extensive with what is knowable, as a kind of knowledge of the second degree, in which it is less a question of learning than of understanding, in which we aim at progressing in depth rather than in extent; not effort to extend the quantity of knowledge, but reflection on the quality of this knowledge. Spontaneous thought — vulgar or scientific — is a direct, simple, and practical thought turned towards things and partial to useful results; seeking what is formulable rather than what is true, or at least so fond of formulæ which can be handled, manipulated, or transmitted, that it is always tempted to see the truth in them; a thought which, moreover, sets out from more or less unguarded postulates, abandons itself to the motive impulses of habits contracted, and goes straight on indefinitely without self-examination. Philosophy, on the contrary, desires to be thought about thought, thought retracing its life and work, knowledge labouring to know itself, fact which aspires to fact about itself, mental effort to become free, to become entirely transparent and luminous in its own eyes, and, if need be, to effect self-reform by dissipating its natural illusions. What we have before our eyes then are the initial postulates themselves, the first spontaneous thoughts, the obscure origins of reason; and we are proceeding towards a point of departure rather than arrival.

The new philosophy does not refuse to carry out this first critical task; but it carries it out in its own way after determining more precisely the real conditions of the problem. At the hour when methodical research begins, the philosopher's mind is not clean-swept; and it would be chimerical to wish to place oneself from the beginning, by some act of transcendence, outside common thought. This thought cannot be inspected and judged from outside. It constitutes, whether we wish it or no, the sole concrete and positive point of departure. Let us add that common-sense constitutes also our sole point of insertion into reality. It can only then be a question of purifying it, not in any way of replacing it. But we must distinguish in it what is *pure fact*, and what is *ulterior arrangement*, in order to see what are the problems which really are presented, and what are, on the contrary, the false problems, the illusory problems, those which relate only to our artifices of language.

The *search for facts* is then the first necessary moment of all philosophy.

But common thought comes before us at the outset as a piece of very composite alluvial ground. It is a beginning of positive science, and also a residue of all philosophical opinions which have had some vogue. That, however, is not its primary basis. *Primum vivere, deinde philosophari*, says the proverb. In certain respects, "speculation is a luxury, whilst action is a necessity."[1] But "life requires us to apprehend things in the relation they have to our needs."[2] Hence comes the

[1] *Creative Evolution*, p. 47.
[2] *Laughter*, p. 154.

IMMEDIACY

fundamental utilitarianism of common-sense. Therefore if we wish to define it in itself and for itself, and no longer as a first approximation of such and such a system of metaphysics, it appears to us no longer as rudimentary science and philosophy, but as an organisation of thought in view of practical life. Thus it is that outside all speculative opinion it is effectively *lived* by all. Its proper language, we may say, is the language of customary perception and mechanical fabrication, therefore a language relative to action, made to express action, modelled upon action, translating things by the relations they maintain to our action; I mean our corporal and synthetic action, which very evidently implies thought, since it is a question of the action of a reasonable being, but which thus contains a thought which is itself eminently practical.

However, we are here regarding common-sense considered as a source of fact. Its utilitarianism then becomes a kind of spontaneous metaphysics from which we must detach ourselves. But is it not the very task of positive science to execute this work of purification? Nothing of the kind, despite appearances and despite intentions. Let us

148   A NEW PHILOSOPHY

examine more closely. The general categories of common thought, according to Mr Bergson,[1] remain those of science; the main roads traced by our senses through the continuity of reality are still those along which science will pass; perception is an infant science and science an adult perception; so much so that customary knowledge and scientific knowledge, both of them destined to prepare our action upon things, are of necessity two visions of the same kind, though of unequal precision and reach. It does not follow that science does not practise a certain disinterestedness as far as immediate mechanical utility is concerned; it does not follow that it has no value as knowledge. But it does not set itself genuinely free from the habits contracted in common experience, and to inform its research it preserves the postulates of common-sense; so that it always grasps things by their "actable" side, by their point of contact with our faculty for action, under the forms by which we handle them conceptually or practically, and all it attains of reality is that by which nature is a possible object of language or industry.

[1] *Philosophic Intuition* in the *Metaphysical and Moral Review*, November 1911, p. 825.

IMMEDIACY 149

Let us turn now towards another aspect of natural thought, to discover in it the germ of the necessary criticism. By the side of "common-sense," which is the first roughdraft of positive science, there is "good sense," which differs from it profoundly, and marks the beginning of what we shall later on call philosophic intuition.[1] It is a sense of what is real, concrete, original, living, an art of equilibrium and precision, a fine touch for complexities, continually feeling like the antennæ of some insects. It contains a certain distrust of the logical faculty in respect of itself; it wages incessant war upon intellectual automatism, upon ready-made ideas and linear deduction; above all, it is anxious to locate and to weigh, without any oversights; it arrests the development of every principle and every method at the precise point where too brutal an application would offend the delicacy of reality; at every moment it collects the whole of our experience and organises it in view of the present. It is, in a word, thought which keeps its freedom, activity which remains awake, suppleness of attitude, attention

[1] *Cf.* an address on *Good Sense and Classical Studies*, delivered by Mr Bergson at the Concours général prize distribution, 30th July 1895.

150 A NEW PHILOSOPHY

to life, an ever-renewed adjustment to suit ever-new situations.

Its revealing virtue is derived from this moving contact with fact, and this living effort of sympathy. This is what we must tend to transpose from the practical to the speculative order.

What, then, will be for us the beginning of philosophy? After taking cognisance of common utilitarianism, and to emerge from the relativity in which it buries us, we seek a departure-point, a criterion, something which decides the raising of inquiry. Where are we to find such a principle, except in the very action of thought; I mean, this time, its action of profound life independent of all practical aim? We shall thus only be imitating the example of Descartes when solving the problem of temporary doubt. What we shall term return to the immediate, the primitive, the pure fact, will be the taking of each perception considered as an act lived, a coloured moment of the *Cogito*, and this will be for us a criterion and departure-point.

Let us specify this point. *Immediate data* or *primitive data* or *pure data* are apprehended by us under forms of disinterested action; I mean that they are first of all lived

this inevitably coincides with a subject directing his organs of aprehension. This is made more clear by Banfield.

rather than conceived, that before becoming *material for science*, they appear as *moments of life*; in brief, that perception of them precedes their use.

It is at this stage previous to language that we are by these pure data in intimate communion with reality itself, and the whole of our critical task is to return to them through a regressive analysis, the goal of which is gradually to make our clear intelligence equal to our primordial intuition. The latter already constitutes a thought, a preconceptual thought which is the intrinsic light of action, which is action itself so far as it is luminous. Thus there is no question here of restricting in any degree the part played by thought, but only of distinguishing between the perceptive and theoretic functions of mind.

What is "the image" of which Mr Bergson speaks at the beginning of *Matter and Mind* except, when grasped in its first movement, the flash of conscious existence "in which the act of knowledge coincides with the generating act of reality"?[1]

Let us forget all philosophical controversies about realism and idealism; let us try to

[1] *Report of the French Philosophical Society*, philosophical vocabulary, article "Immediate."

reconstruct for ourselves a simplicity, a virginal and candid glance, freeing us from the habits contracted in the course of practical life. These then are our "images": not things presented externally, nor states felt internally, not portraits of exterior beings nor projections of internal moods, but *appearances*, in the etymological sense of the word, appearances lived simply, without our being distinguished from them, as yet neither subjective nor objective, marking a moment of consciousness previous to the work of reflection, from which proceeds the duality of subject and object. And such also, in every order, appear the "immediate feelings"; as action in birth, previous to language.[1]

Why depart from the immediate thus conceived as action and life? Because it is quite impossible to do otherwise, for every initial fact can be only such a pulsation of consciousness in its lived act, and the fundamental and primitive direction of the least word, were it in an enunciation of a problem or a doubt, can only be such a direction of life and action. And we must certainly accord to this immediacy a value of absolute knowledge, since it realises the coincidence of being and knowledge.

[1] *Cf. Matter and Memory,* Foreword to the 7th edition.

IMMEDIACY

But let us not think that the perception of immediacy is simple passive perception, that it is sufficient to open our eyes to obtain it, to-day when our utilitarian education is completed and has passed into the state of habit. There is a difference between common experience and the initial action of life; the first is a practical limitation of the second. Hence it follows that a previous criticism is necessary to return from one to the other, a criticism always in activity, always open as a way of progressive investigation, always ready for the reiteration and the renewal of effort.

In this task of purification there is doubtless always to be feared an illusion of remaining in the primitive stage. By what criteria, by what signs can we recognise that we have touched the goal? Pure fact is shown to be such on the one hand because it remains independent of all theoretical symbolism, because the critique of language allows it to exist thus as an indissoluble residue, because we are unable not to "live" it, even when we free ourselves from the anxiety of utility; on the other hand, because it dominates all systems, and imposes itself equally upon them all as the common source from which they derive by diverging analyses, and in which they become reconciled. Assuredly, to attain it, to extricate it, we must appeal to the revelations of science, to the exercise of deliberate thought. But this employment of analysis against analysis does not in any way constitute a circle, for it tends only to destroy prejudices which have become unconscious: it is a simple artifice destined to break off habits and to scatter illusions by changing the points of view. Once set free, once again become capable of direct and simple view, what we accept as fact is what bears no trace of synthetic elaboration. It is true that here a last objection presents itself: how shall we think this limit, purely given, to any degree at all in fact, if it must precede all language?

The answer is easy. Why speak thus of limit? This word has two senses: at one time it designates a last term in a series of approximations, and at another a certain internal character of convergence, a certain quality of progression.

Now, it is the second sense only which suits the case before us. Immediacy contains no matter statically defined, and no thing. The notion of fact is quite relative. What is *fact* in one case may become *construction* in another. For example, the percepts of common experience are facts for the physicist, and constructions for the philosopher; the same applies to a table of numerical results, for the scholar who is trying to establish a theory, or for the observer and the psychologist. We may then conceive a series in which each term is fact in relation to those which follow it, and constructed in relation to those which precede it. The expression "primitive fact" then determines not so much a final object as a direction of thought, a movement of critical retrogression, a journey from the most to the least elaborate, and the "contact with pure immediacy" is only the effort, more and more prolonged, to convert the elements of experience into real and profound action.

III
THEORY OF PERCEPTION

OF what the work of return to immediacy consists, and how the intuition which it calls up reveals absolute fact, we shall see by an example, if we study more closely a capital point of Mr Bergson's philosophy, the theory of external perception.

If the act of perceiving realises the lived communion of the subject and object in the image, we must admit that here we have the perfect knowledge which we wish to obtain always: we resign ourselves to conception only for want of perception, and our ideal is to convert all conception into perception. Doubtless we might define philosophy by this same ideal, as an effort to expand our perceptive power until we render it capable of grasping all the wealth and all the depth of reality at a single glance. Too true it is that such an ideal remains inaccessible to us. Something, however, is given us already in æsthetic intuition. Mr Bergson has pointed it out in some admirable pages,[1] and has explained to us also how philosophy pursues an analogous end.[2]

But philosophy must be conceived as an art implying science and criticism, all experience and all reason. It is when we look at metaphysics in this way that they become a positive order of veritable knowledge. Kant has conclusively established that what lies beyond language can only be attained by direct vision, not by dialectic progress. His mistake was that he afterwards believed such a vision for ever impossible; and whence did this mistake arise, if not from the fact that, for his new vision, he exacted intuitive faculties quite different from those at man's disposal. Here again the artist will be our example and model. He appeals to no transcendent sense, but detaches common-sense from its utilitarian prejudices. Let us do the same: we shall obtain a similar result without laying ourselves open to Kant's objections. This work is everywhere possible, and it is, *par excellence*, the work of

[1] *Laughter*, pp. 153–161.
[2] First lecture on *The Perception of Change*, delivered at Oxford, 26th May 1911.

philosophy: let us try then to sketch it in relation to the perception of matter.

We must distinguish two senses of the word "perception." This word means first of all *simple apprehension of immediacy, grasp of primitive fact.* When we use it in this sense, we will agree to say *pure perception.* It is perhaps in place to see in it nothing but a limit which concrete experience never presents unmixed, a direction of research rather than the possession of a thing.

However that may be, the first sense is the fundamental sense, and what it designates must be at the root of all *ordinary perception*; I mean, of every mental operation which results in the construction of a *percept*: a term formed by analogy with *concept*, representing the result of a complex work of analysis and synthesis, with judgment from externals. We live the images in an act of pure perception, whilst the objects of ordinary perception are, for example, the bodies of which we speak in common language.

With regard to the relation of the two senses which we have just distinguished, common opinion seems very precise. It might be thus resumed: at the point of departure we have simple sensations, similar

THEORY OF PERCEPTION 159

to qualitative atoms (this is the part of pure perception), and afterwards their arrangement into connected systems, which are percepts.

But criticism does not authorise this manner of looking at it. Nowhere does knowledge begin by separate elements. Such elements are always a product of analysis. So there is a problem to solve to regain the basis of pure perception which is hidden and obscured by our familiar percepts.

Do not suppose that the solution of this problem is easy. One method only is of any use: to plunge into reality, to become immersed in it, in a long-pursued effort to assimilate all the records of common-sense and positive science. "For we do not obtain an intuition of reality, that is to say, an intellectual sympathy with its inmost content, unless we have gained its confidence by long companionship with its superficial manifestations. And it is not a question merely of assimilating the leading facts; we must accumulate and melt them down into such an enormous mass that we are sure, in this fusion, of neutralising in one another all the preconceived and premature ideas which observers may have unconsciously allowed to form the sediment of their observations.

Thus, and only thus, is crude materiality to be disengaged from known facts."[1]

A directing principle controls this work and reintroduces order and convergence, after dispensing with them at the outset; viz. that, contrary to common opinion, perception as practised in the course of daily life, "natural" perception does not aim at a goal of disinterested knowledge, but one of practical utility, or rather, if it is knowledge, it is only knowledge elaborated in view of action and speech.

Need we repeat here the proofs by which we have already established in the most positive manner that such is really the meaning of ordinary perception, the underlying reason which causes it to take the place of pure perception? We perceive by habit only what is useful to us, what interests us practically; very often, too, we think we are perceiving when we are merely inferring, as for example when we seem to *see* a dis-

[1] *Introduction to Metaphysics* in the *Metaphysical and Moral Review*, January 1903. For the correct interpretation of this passage ("intellectual sympathy") it must not be forgotten that before *Creative Evolution,* Mr Bergson employed the word "intelligence" in a wider acceptation, more akin to that commonly received.

THEORY OF PERCEPTION 161

tance in depth, a succession of planes, of which in reality we *judge* by differences of colouring or relief.

Our senses supplement one another. A slow education has gradually taught us to co-ordinate their impressions, especially those of touch to those of vision.[1]

Theoretical forms come between nature and us: a veil of symbols envelops reality; thus, finally, we no longer see things themselves, we are content to read the labels on them.

Moreover, our perception appears to analysis completely saturated with memories, and that in view of our practical insertion in the present. I will not come back to this point which has been so lucidly explained by Mr Bergson in a lecture on *Dream*[2] and an article on *Intellectual Effort*,[3] the reading of which cannot be too strongly recommended as an introduction to the first chapter of *Matter and Memory*, in which further arguments are to be found. I will only add one remark, follow-

[1] H. Bergson, *Note on the Psychological Origins of Our Belief in the Law of Causality.* Vol. i. of the *Library of the International Philosophical Congress*, 1900.

[2] *Report of the International Psychological Institute*, May 1901.

[3] *Philosophical Review*, January 1902.

11

ing Mr Bergson, as always: perception is not simply contemplation, but consciousness of an original visual emotion combined with a complete group of actions in embryo, gestures in outline, and the graze of movement within, by which we prepare to grasp the object, describe its lines, test its functions, sound it, move it, and handle it in a thousand ways.[1]

From the preceding observations springs the utilitarian and practical nature of common perception. Let us attempt now to see of what the elaboration which it makes reality undergo consists. This time I am summing up the fourth chapter of *Matter and Memory*. First of all, we choose between the images, emphasising the strong, extinguishing the weak, although both have, *a priori*, the same interest for pure knowledge; we make this choice above all by according preference to impressions of touch, which are the most useful from the practical point of view. This selection determines the parcelling up of matter into independent bodies, and the artificial character of our proceeding is thus made plain. Does not science, indeed, conclude in the same

[1] This is attested by the facts of *apraxia* or *psychic blindness*. *Cf. Matter and Memory*, chap. ii.

way, showing us—as soon as she frees herself even to a small extent from common-sense —full continuity re-established by " moving strata," and all bodies resolved into stationary waves and knots of intersecting fluxes? Already, then, we shall be nearer pure perception if we cease to consider anything but the perceptible stuff in which numerically distinct percepts are cut. Even there, however, a utilitarian division continues. Our senses are instruments of abstraction, each of them discerning a possible path of action. We may say that corporal life functions in the manner of an absorbing *milieu*, which determines the disconnected scale of simple qualities by extinguishing most of the perceptible radiations. In short, the scale of sensations, with its numerical aspect, is nothing but the spectrum of our practical activity. Commonly we perceive only averages and wholes, which we contract into distinct " qualities." Let us disengage from this rhythm what is peculiar to ourselves.

Above all, let us strive to disengage ourselves from homogeneous space, this substratum of fixity, this arbitrary scheme of measurement and division, which, to our greater advantage, subtends the natural, qualitative, and undivided extension of images.[1] And we shall finally have pure perception in so far as it is accessible to us.

There is no disputing the absolute value of this pure perception. The impotence of speculative reason, as demonstrated by Kant, is perhaps, at bottom, only the impotence of an intelligence in bondage to certain necessities of the corporal life, and exercised upon a matter which it has had to disorganise for the satisfaction of our needs. Our knowledge of things is then no longer relative to the fundamental structure of our mind, but only to its superficial and acquired habits, to the contingent form which it takes on from our corporal functions and our lower needs.

The relativity of knowledge is therefore not final. In unmaking what our needs have made we re-establish intuition in its original purity, and resume contact with reality.[2]

That is how things are really presented. Here we are confronted by the moving con-

---

[1] We usually represent homogeneous space as previous to the heterogeneous extension of images: as a kind of *empty room* which we *furnish* with percepts. We must reverse this order, and conceive, on the contrary, that extension precedes space.

[2] *Matter and Memory*, p. 203.

tinuity of images. Pure perception is complete perception. From it we pass to ordinary perception by diminution, throwing shadows here and there: the reality perceived by commonsense is nothing else actually than universal interaction rendered visible by its very interruption at certain points.

Whence we have this double conclusion already formulated higher up: *the relation of perception to matter is that of the part to the whole, and our consciousness is rather limited than relative.* It must be stated that primarily we perceive things in themselves, not in us; the subjectivity of our current perception comes from our work of outlining it in the bosom of reality, but the root of pure perception plunges into full objectivity. If, at each point of matter, we were to succeed in possessing the stream of total interaction of which it marks a wave, and if we were to succeed in seeing the multiplicity of these points as a qualitative heterogeneous flux without number or severance, we should coincide with reality itself. It is true that such an ideal, while inaccessible on the one hand, would not succeed on the other without risk to knowledge; in fact, says Mr Bergson,[1] "to

[1] *Matter and Memory*, p. 38.

perceive all the influences of all the points of all bodies would be to descend to the state of material object."

But a solution of this double difficulty remains possible, a dynamic and approximate solution, which consists in looking for the absolute intuition of matter in such a mobilisation of our perspective faculties that we become capable of following, according to the circumstances, all the paths of virtual perception of which the common anxiety for the practical has made us choose one only, and capable of realising all the infinitely different modes of *qualification* and *discernment*.

But we have still to see how this " complete experience " can be practically thought.

IV
CRITIQUE OF LANGUAGE

THE perception of reality does not obtain the full value of knowledge, except when once socialised, once made the common property of men, and thereby also tested and verified.

There is one means only of doing that; viz. to analyse it into manageable and portable concepts. By language I mean the product of this conceptualisation. Thus language is necessary; for we must always speak, were it only to utter the impotence of words. Not less necessary is a critique of spontaneous language, of the laws which govern it, of the postulates which it embraces, of the methods which convey its implicit doctrines. Synthetic forms are actually *theories* already; they effect an adaptation of reality to the demands of practical use. If it is impossible to escape them, it is at least fitting not to employ them except with due knowledge, and when properly warned against the illusion of the false problems which they might arouse.

Let us first of all consider thought in itself, in its concrete life. What are the principal characteristics, the essential steps ? We readily say, analysis and synthesis.

Nothing can be known except in contrast, correlation, or negation of another thing; and the act of knowledge, considered in itself, is unification. Thus number appears as a fundamental category, as an absolute condition of intelligibility; some go so far as to regard atomism as a necessary method. But that is inexact. No doubt the use of number and the resulting atomism are imposed by definition, we might say, on the thought which proceeds by conceptual analysis, and then by unifying construction; that is to say, on synthetic thought. But, in greater depth, thought is *dynamic continuity* and *duration*. Its essential work does not consist in discerning and afterwards in assembling ready-made elements. Let us see in it rather a kind of creative maturation, and let us attempt to grasp the nature of this causal activity.[1]

The act of thought is always a complex play

[1] H. Bergson, *Intellectual Effort* in the *Philosophical Review*, January 1902.

of moving representations, an evolution of life in which incessant inner reactions occur. That is to say, it is movement. But there are several planes of thought, from intuition to language, and we must distinguish between the thought which moves on the surface among terms displayed on a single plane, and the thought which goes deeper and deeper from one plane to another.

We do not think solely by concepts or images; we think, first of all, according to Mr Bergson's expression, by *dynamic schemes*. What is a dynamic scheme? It is motive rather than representative, inexpressible in itself, but a source of language containing not so much the images or concepts in which it will develop as the indication of the path to be followed in order to obtain them. It is not so much system as movement, progress, genesis; it does not mark the gaze directed upon the various points of one plane of deliberate contemplation so much as an effort to pass through successive planes of thought in a direction leading from intuition to analysis. We might define it by its function of calling up images and concepts, representations which, for one and the same scheme, are neither strictly determined nor anything in particular in themselves, concurrent representations which have in common one and the same logical power.

The representations called up form a body to the scheme, and the relation of the scheme to the concepts and images which it calls up resembles, *mutatis mutandis*, the relation pointed out by Mr Bergson between an idea and its basis in the brain. In short, it is the very act of creative thought which the dynamic scheme interprets, the act not yet fixed in "results."

Nothing is easier than to illustrate the existence of this scheme. Let us merely remark a few facts of current observation. Recall, for example, the suggestive anxiety we experience when we seek to remember a name; the precise syllables of the name still escape us, but we feel them approaching, and already we possess something of them, since we immediately reject those which do not answer to a certain direction of expectancy; and by endeavouring to secure a more intimate feeling of this direction we suddenly arouse the desired recollection.

In the same way, what does it mean to have the sense of a complex situation in active life, if not that we perceive it, not as a static group of explicit details, but as a meeting of powers

CRITIQUE OF LANGUAGE 171

allied or hostile, convergent or divergent, directed towards this or that, of which the aggregate whole tends of itself to awaken in us the initial reactions which analyse it?

In the same way again, how do we learn, how can we assimilate a vast system of concepts or images? Our task is not to concentrate an enumerative attention on each individual factor; we should never get away from them, the weight would be too heavy.

What we entrust to memory is really a dynamic scheme permitting us to "regain" what we should not have succeeded in "retaining." In reality our only "knowledge" is through such a scheme, which contains in the state of potential implication an inexhaustible multiplicity ready to be developed in actual representations.

How, finally, is any discovery made? Finding is solving a problem; and to solve a problem we must always begin by supposing it solved. But of what does such a hypothesis consist?

It is not an anticipated view of the solution, for then all would be at an end; nor is it a simple formula putting in the present indicative what the enunciation expressed in the future or the imperative, for then nothing would be begun. It is exactly a dynamic scheme; that is to say, a method in the state of directed tension; and often, the discovery once realised as theory or system, capable of unending developments and resurrections, remains by the best of itself a method and a dynamic scheme.

But one last example will perhaps reveal the truth still more. " Anyone who has attempted literary composition knows well that when the subject has been long studied, all the documents collected, all the notes taken, we need, to embark on the actual work of composition, something more, an effort, often very painful, to place oneself suddenly in the very heart of the subject, and to seek as deep down as possible an impulse to which afterwards we shall only have to let ourselves go. This impulse, once received, projects the mind on a road where it finds both the information which it had collected and a thousand other details as well; it develops and analyses itself in terms, the enumeration of which would have no end; the further we advance, the more we discover; we shall never succeed in saying everything; and yet, if we turn sharply round towards the impulse we feel behind ourselves, to grasp it, it escapes; for it was not a thing but a direction of movement, and though indefinitely extensible, it is simplicity itself."[1]

The thought, then, which proceeds from one representation to another in one and the same plane is one kind; that which follows one and the same conceptual direction through descending planes is another. Creative and fertile thought is the thought which adopts the second kind of work. The ideal is a continual oscillation from one plane to the other, a restless alternative of intuitive concentration and conceptual expansion. But our idleness takes exception to this, for the feeling of effort appears precisely in the traject from the dynamic scheme to the images and concepts, in the passing from one plane of thought to another.

Thus the natural tendency is to remain in the last of these planes, that of language. We know what dangers threaten us there.

Suppose we have some idea or other and the word representing it. Do not suppose that to this word there is one corresponding sense only, nor even a finished group of various distinct and rigorously separable senses. On

[1] H. Bergson, *Metaphysical and Moral Review*, January 1903. The whole critique of language is implicitly contained in this *Introduction to Metaphysics*.

the contrary, there is a whole scale corresponding, a complete continuous spectrum of unstable meanings which tend unceasingly to resolve into one another. Dictionaries attempt to illuminate them. The task is impossible. They co-ordinate a few guiding marks; but who shall say what infinite transitions underlie them?

A word designates rather a current of thought than one or several halts on a logical path. Here again a dynamic continuity exists previous to the parcelling out of the acceptations. What, then, should be the attitude of mind?

A supple moving attitude more attentive to the curve of change than to the possible halting-points along the road. But this is not the case at all; the effort would be too great, and what happens, on the contrary, is this. For the spectrum a chromatic scale of uniform tints is very quickly substituted. This is in itself an undesirable simplification, for it is impossible to reconstitute the infinity of real shades by combinations of fundamental colours each representing the homogeneous shore, which each region of the spectrum finally becomes.

However cleverly we proportion these averages, we get, at most, some vulgar counterfeit:

CRITIQUE OF LANGUAGE 175

orange, for example, *is* not a mixture of yellow and red, although this mixture may *recall* to those who have known it elsewhere the simple and original sensation of orange. Again, a second simplification, still more undesirable, succeeds the first.

There are no longer any colours at all; black lines serve as guide-marks. We are therefore with pure concepts decidedly in full symbolism. And it is with symbols that we shall henceforward be trying to reconstruct reality.

I need not go back to the general characteristics or the inconveniences of this method. Concepts resemble photographic views; concrete thickness escapes them. However exact, varied, or numerous we suppose them, they can certainly *recall* their object, but not *reveal* it to any one who had not had any direct intuition of it. Nothing is easier than to trace the plan of a body in four dimensions; all the same, this drawing does not admit "visualisation in space" as is the case with ordinary bodies, for want of a previous intuition which it would awaken: thus it is with concepts in relation to reality. Like photographs and like plans, they are *extracted* from reality, but we are not able to say that they were *contained* in it; and many of them besides are not so much as extracts; they are simple systematised notes, in fact, notes made upon notes. In other terms, concepts do not represent pieces, parts, or elements of reality. Literally they are nothing but simple symbolic notations. To wish to make integral factors of them would be as strange an illusion as that of seeing in the co-ordinates of a geometric point the constitutive essence of that point.

We do not make things with symbols, any more than we should reconstruct a picture with the qualifications which classify it.

Whence, then, comes the natural inclination of thought towards the concept? From the fact that thought delights in artifices which facilitate analysis and language.

The first of these artifices is that from which results the possibility of decomposition or recomposition according to arbitrary laws. For that we need a previous substitution of symbols for things. Nothing demonstrates this better than the celebrated arguments which we owe to Zeno of Elea. Mr Bergson returns to the discussion of them over and over again.[1]

---

[1] *Essay on the Immediate Data,* pp. 85–86; *Matter and Memory,* pp. 211–213; *Creative Evolution,* pp. 333–337.

The nerve of the reasoning there consists in the evident absurdity there would be in conceiving an inexhaustible exhausted, an unachievable achieved; in short, a total actually completed, and yet obtained by the successive addition of an infinite number of terms.

But the question is to know whether a movement can be considered as a numerical multiplicity. Virtual divisibility there is, no doubt, but not actual division; divisibility is indefinite, whereas an actual division, if it respects the inner articulations of reality, is bound to halt at a limited number of phases.

What we divide and measure is the track of the movement once accomplished, not the movement itself: it is the trajectory, not the traject. In the trajectory we can count endless positions; that is to say, possible halts. Let us not suppose that the moving body meets these elements all ready-marked. Hence what the Eleatic dialectic illustrates is a case of incommensurability; the radical inability of analysis to end a certain task; our powerlessness to explain the fact of the transit, if we apply to it such and such modes of numerical decomposition or recomposition, which are valid only for space; the impossibility of conceiving becoming as susceptible of being cut up into arbitrary segments, and afterwards reconstructed by summing of terms according to some law or other; in short, it is the nature of movement, which is without division, number, or concept.

But thought delights in analyses regulated by the sole consideration of easy language; hence its tendency to an arithmetic and geometry of concepts, in spite of the disastrous consequences; and thus the Eleatic paradox is no less instructive in its specious character than in the solution which it embodies.

At bottom, natural thought, I mean thought which abandons itself to its double inclination of synthetic idleness and useful industry, is a thought haunted by anxieties of the operating manual, anxieties of fabrication.

What does it care about the fluxes of reality and dynamic depths? It is only interested in the outcrops scattered here and there over the firm soil of the practical, and it solidifies "terms" like stakes plunged in a moving ground. Hence comes the configuration of its spontaneous logic to a geometry of solids, and hence come concepts, the instantaneous moments taken in transitions.

Scientific thought, again, preserves the same

habits and the same preferences. It seeks only what repeats, what can be counted. Everywhere, when it theorises, it tends to establish static relations between composing unities which form a homogeneous and disconnected multiplicity.

Its very instruments bias it in that direction. The apparatus of the laboratory really grasps nothing but arrangement and coincidence ; in a word, states not transitions. Even in cases of contrary appearance, for example, when we determine a weight by observing the oscillation of a balance and not its rest, we are interested in regular recurrence, in a symmetry, in something therefore which is of the nature of an equilibrium and a fixity all the same. The reason of it is that science, like common-sense, although in a manner a little different, aims only in actual fact at obtaining finished and workable *results*.

Let us imagine reality under the figure of a curve, a rhythmic succession of phases of which our concepts mark so many tangents. There is contact at one point, but at one point only. Thus our logic is valid as infinitesimal analysis, just as the geometry of the straight line allows us to define each state of curve. It is thus, for example, that vitality maintains a relation of momentary tangency to the physico-chemical structure. If we study this relation and analogous relations, this fact remains indisputably legitimate. Let us not think, however, that such a study, even when repeated in as many points as we wish, can ever suffice.

We must afterwards by genuine integration attain moving continuity. That is exactly the task represented by the return to intuition, with its proper instrument, the dynamic scheme. From this tangential point of view we try to grasp the genesis of the curve as envelope, or rather, and better still, the birth of successive tangents as instantaneous directions. Speaking non-metaphorically, we cling to genetic methods of conceptualisation and proceed from the generating principle to its conceptual derivatives.

But our thought finds it very difficult to sustain such an effort long. It is partial to rectilineal deduction, actual becoming horrifies it. It desires immediately to find "things" sharply determined and very clear. That is why immediately a tangent is constructed, it follows its movement in a straight line to infinity. Thus are produced *limit-concepts*, the ultimate terms, the atoms of language.

As a rule they go in pairs, in antithetic couples, every analysis being dichotomy, since the discernment of one path of abstraction determines in contrast, as a complementary remainder, the opposite path of direction. Hence, according to the selection effected among concepts, and the relative weight which is attributed to them, we get the antinomies between which a philosophy of analysis must for ever remain oscillating and torn in sunder. Hence comes the parcelling up of metaphysics into systems, and its appearance of regulated play " between antagonistic schools which get up on the stage together, each to win applause in turn."[1]

The method followed to find a genuine solution must be inverse; not dialectic combination of pre-existing concepts, but, setting out from a direct and really lived intuition, a descent to ever new concepts along dynamic schemes which remain open. From the same intuition spring many concepts: "As the wind which rushes into the crossroads divides into diverging currents of air, which are all only one and the same gust."[2]

[1] H. Bergson, *Report of the French Philosophical Society*, meeting, 2nd May 1901.
[2] *Creative Evolution*, p. 55.

182 A NEW PHILOSOPHY

The antinomies are resolved genetically, whilst in the plane of language they remain irreducible. With a heterogeneity of shades, when we mix the tints and neutralise them by one another, we easily create homogeneity; but take the result of this work, that is to say, the average final colour, and it will be impossible to reconstitute the wealth of the original.

Do you desire a precise example of the work we must accomplish? Take that of change;[1] no other is more significant or clearer. It shows us two necessary movements in the reform of our habits of imagination or conception.

Let us try first of all to familiarise ourselves with the images which show us the fixity deriving from becoming.

Two colliding waves, two rollers meeting, typify rest by extinction and interference. With the movement of a stone, and the fluidity of running water, we form the instantaneous position of a ricochet. The very movement of the stone, seen in the successive positions of the tangent to the trajectory, is stationary to our view.

What is dynamic stability, except non-

[1] *Cf.* two lectures delivered by Mr Bergson at Oxford on *The Perception of Change*, 26th and 27th May 1911.

CRITIQUE OF LANGUAGE 183

variation arising from variation itself? Equilibrium is produced from speed. A man running solidifies the moving ground. In short, two moving bodies regulated by each other become fixed in relation to each other.

After this, let us try to perceive change in itself, and then represent it to ourselves according to its specific and original nature.

The common conception needs reform on two principal points:

(1) All change is revealed in the light of immediate intuition, not as a numerical series of states, but a rhythm of phases, each of which constitutes an indivisible act, in such a way that each change has its natural inner articulations, forbidding us to break it up according to arbitrary laws, like a homogeneous length.

(2) Change is self-sufficient; it has no need of a support, a moving body, a "thing" in motion. There is no vehicle, no substance, no spatial receptacle, resembling a theatre-scene, no material dummy successively draped in coloured stuffs; on the contrary, it is the body or the atom which should be subordinately defined as symbols of completed becoming.

Of movement thus conceived, indivisible and

substantial, what better image can we have than a musical evolution, a phrase in melody? That is how we must work to conceive reality. If such a conception at first appears obscure, let us credit experience, for ideas are gradually illuminated by the very use we make of them, "the clarity of a concept being hardly anything, at bottom, but the assurance once obtained that we can handle it profitably."[1]

If we require to reach a conception of this kind with regard to change, the Eleatic dialectic is there to establish it beyond dispute, and positive science comes to the same conclusion, since it shows us everywhere nothing but movements placed upon movements, never fixed "things," except as temporary symbols of what we leave at a given moment outside the field of study.

In any case, the difficulty of such a conception need not stop us; it is little more than a difficulty of the imaginative order. And as for the conception itself, or rather the corresponding intuition, it will share the fate of all its predecessors: to our contemporaries it will be a scandal, a century later a stroke of genius, after some centuries common evidence, and finally an instinctive axiom.

[1] H. Bergson, *Introduction to Metaphysics*.

V
THE PROBLEM OF CONSCIOUSNESS. DURATION AND LIBERTY

ARMED with the method we have just described, Mr Bergson turned first of all toward the problem of the ego : taking up his position in the centre of mind, he has attempted to establish its independent reality by examining its profound nature.

The first chapter of the *Essay on the Immediate Data* contains a decisive criticism of the conceptions which claim to introduce number and measure into the domain of the facts of consciousness.

Not that it is our business to reject as false the notion of psychological intensity ; but this notion demands interpretation, and the least that we can say against the attempt to turn it into a notion of size is that in doing so we are misunderstanding the specific character of the object studied. The same reproach must be levelled against *association of ideas*, the system of mechanical psychology of which the type is presented us by Taine and Stuart Mill. Already in chaps. ii. and iii. of the *Essay*, and again all through *Matter and Memory*, the system is riddled with objections, each of which would be sufficient to show its radical flaw. All the aspects, all the phenomena of mental life come up for successive review. In respect of each of them we have an illustration of the insufficiency of the atomism which seeks to recompose the soul with fixed elements, by a massing of units exterior to one another, everywhere and always the same: this is a grammatical philosophy which believes reality to be composed of parts which admit of number just as language is made of words placed side by side; it is a materialist philosophy which improperly transfers the proceedings of the physical sciences to the sciences of the inner life.

On the contrary, we must represent the state of consciousness to ourselves as variable according to the whole of which it forms a part. Here and there, although it always bears the same name, it is no longer the same thing. "The more the ego becomes itself again, the more also do its states of consciousness, instead of being in juxtaposition, penetrate one another, blend with one another, and tinge one another with the colouring of all the rest. Thus each of us has his manner of loving or hating, and this love or hate reflect our entire personality."[1]

At bottom Mr Bergson is bringing forward the necessity, in the case before us, of substituting a new notion of continuous qualitative heterogeneity for the old notion of numerical and spatial continuity. Above all, he is emphasising the still more imperious necessity of regarding each state as a phase in duration; and we are here touching on his principal and leading intuition, the intuition of real duration.

Historically this was Mr Bergson's starting-point and the origin of his thought: a criticism of time under the form in which common-sense imagines it, in which science employs it. He was the first to notice the fact that scientific time has no "duration." Our equations really express only static relations between simultaneous phenomena; even the differential quotients they may contain in reality mark nothing but *present* tendencies; no change would take place in our calculations

[1] *Essay on the Immediate Data*, pp. 125–126.

if the time were given in advance, instantaneously fulfilled, like a linear whole of points in numerical order, with no more genuine duration than that contained in the numerical succession. Even in astronomy there is less anticipation than judgment of constancy and stability, the phenomena being almost strictly periodic, while the hazard of prediction bears only upon the minute divergence between the actual phenomenon and the exact period attributed to it. Notice under what figure common-sense imagines time: as an inert receptacle, a homogeneous *milieu*, neutral and indifferent; in fact, a kind of space.

The scholar makes use of a like image; for he defines time by its measurement, and all measurement implies interpretation in space. For the scholar the hour is not an interval, but a coincidence, an instantaneous arrangement, and time is resolved into a dust of fixities, as in those pneumatic clocks in which the hand moves forward in jerks, marking nothing but a sequence of pauses.

Such symbols are sufficient, at least for a first approximation, when it is only a question of matter, the mechanism of which, strictly considered, contains nothing " durable." But in biology and psychology quite different characteristics become essential; age and memory, heterogeneity of musical phases, irreversible rhythm "which cannot be lengthened or shortened at will."[1]

Then it is that the return of *time* becomes necessary to *duration*. How are we to describe this duration? It is a melodious evolution of moments, each of which contains the resonance of those preceding and announces the one which is going to follow; it is a process of enriching which never ceases, and a perpetual appearance of novelty; it is an indivisible, qualitative, and organic becoming, foreign to space, refractory to number.

Summon the image of a stream of consciousness passing through the continuity of the spectrum, and becoming tinged successively with each of its shades. Or rather imagine a symphony having feeling of itself, and creating itself; that is how we should conceive duration.

That duration thus conceived is really the basis of ourselves Mr Bergson proves by a thousand examples, and by a marvellous employment of the introspective method which he has helped to make so popular. We cannot quote these admirable analyses here.

[1] *Creative Evolution*, p. 10.

A single one will serve as model, specially selected as referring to one of the most ordinary moments of our life, to show plainly that the perception of real duration always accompanies us in secret.

"At the moment when I write these lines a clock near me is striking the hour; but my distracted ear is only aware of it after several strokes have already sounded; that is, I have not counted them. And yet an effort of introspective attention enables me to total the four strokes already struck and add them to those which I hear. If I then withdraw into myself and carefully question myself about what has just happened, I become aware that the first four sounds had struck my ear and even moved my consciousness, but that the sensations produced by each of them, instead of following in juxtaposition, had blended into one another in such a way as to endow the whole with a peculiar aspect and make of it a kind of musical phrase. In order to estimate in retrospect the number of strokes which have sounded, I attempted to reconstitute this phrase in thought: my imagination struck one, then two, then three, and so long as it had not reached the exact number four, my sensibility, on being

THE PROBLEM OF CONSCIOUSNESS 191

questioned, replied that the total effect differed in quality. It had therefore noted the succession of the four strokes in a way of its own, but quite otherwise than by addition, and without bringing in the image of a juxtaposition of distinct terms. In fact, the number of strokes struck was perceived as quality, not as quantity: duration is thus presented to immediate consciousness, and preserves this form so long as it does not give place to a symbolical representation drawn from space."[1]

And now are we to believe that return to the feeling of real duration consists in letting ourselves go, and allowing ourselves an idle relaxation in dream or dissolution in sensation, "as a shepherd dozing watches the water flow"? Or are we even to believe, as has been maintained, that the intuition of duration reduces "to the spasm of delight of the mollusc basking in the sun"? This is a complete mistake! We should fall back into the misconceptions which I was pointing out in connection with immediacy in general; we should be forgetting that there are several rhythms of duration, as there are several kinds of consciousness; and finally, we should be misunderstanding the

[1] *Essay on the Immediate Data*, pp. 95-96.

character of a creative invention perpetually renewed, which is that of our inner life.

For it is in duration that we are free, not in spatialised time, as all determinist conceptions suppose in contradiction.

I shall not go back to the proofs of this thesis; they were condensed some way back after the third chapter of the *Essay on the Immediate Data*. But I will borrow from Mr Bergson himself a few complementary explanations, in order, as far as possible, to forestall any misunderstanding. "The word *liberty*," he says, "has for me a sense intermediate between those which we assign as a rule to the two terms liberty and free-will. On one hand, I believe that liberty consists in being entirely oneself, in acting in conformity with oneself; it is then, to a certain degree, the 'moral liberty' of philosophers, the independence of the person with regard to everything other than itself. But that is not quite this liberty, since the independence I am describing has not always a moral character. Further, it does not consist in depending on oneself as an effect depends on the cause which *of necessity* determines it. In this, I should come back to the sense of 'free-will.' And yet I do not accept this sense completely either, since free-

THE PROBLEM OF CONSCIOUSNESS 193

will, in the usual meaning of the term, implies the equal possibility of two contraries, and on my theory we cannot formulate, or even conceive in this case the thesis of the equal possibility of the two contraries, without falling into grave error about the nature of time. I might say then, that the object of my thesis, on this particular point, has been precisely to find a position intermediate between 'moral liberty' and 'free-will.' *Liberty*, such as I understand it, is situated between these two terms, but not at equal distances from both. If I were obliged to blend it with one of the two, I should select 'free-will.'"[1]

After all, when we place ourselves in the perspective of homogeneous time; that is to say, when we substitute for the real and profound ego its image refracted through space, the act necessarily appears either as the resultant of a mechanical composition of elements, or as an incomprehensible creation *ex nihilo*.

"We have supposed that there is a third course to pursue; that is, to place ourselves back in pure duration. . . . Then we seemed to see action arise from its antecedents by an

[1] *Report of the French Philosophical Society*, philosophical vocabulary, article "Liberty."

evolution *sui generis*, in such a way that we discover in this action the antecedents which explain it, while at the same time it adds something absolutely new to them, being an advance upon them as the fruit upon the flower. Liberty is in no way reduced thereby, as has been said, to obvious spontaneity. At most this would be the case in the animal world, where the psychological life is principally that of the affections. But in the case of man, a thinking being, the free act can be called a synthesis of feelings and ideas, and the evolution which leads to it a reasonable evolution."[1]

Finally, in a most important letter,[2] Mr Bergson becomes a little more precise still. We must certainly not confuse the affirmation of liberty with the negation of physical determinism; "for there is *more* in this affirmation than in this negation." All the same, liberty supposes a certain contingence. It is "psychological causality itself," which must not be represented after the model of physical causality.

In opposition to the latter, it implies that

[1] *Matter and Memory*, p. 205.
[2] *Report of the French Philosophical Society*, meeting, 26th February 1903.

between two moments of a conscious being there is not an equivalence admitting of deduction, that in the transition from one to the other there is a genuine creation. Without doubt the free act is not without explanatory reasons.

"But these reasons have determined us only at the moment when they have become determining; that is, at the moment when the act was virtually accomplished, and the creation of which I speak is entirely contained in the *progress* by which these reasons *have become* determining." It is true that all this implies a certain independence of mental life in relation to the mechanism of matter; and that is why Mr Bergson was obliged to set himself the problem of the relations between body and mind.

We know that the solution of this problem is the principal object of *Matter and Memory*. The thesis of psycho-physiological parallelism is there peremptorily refuted.

The method which Mr Bergson has followed to do so will be found set out by himself in a communication to the *French Philosophical Society*, which it is important to study as introduction.[1] The paralogism included in the

[1] *Report* of meeting, 2nd May 1901.

very enunciation of the parallelist thesis is explained in a *mémoire* presented to the *Geneva International Philosophical Congress* in 1904.[1] But the actual proof is made by the analysis of the *mémoire* which fills chaps. ii. and iii. of the work cited above.[2] It is there established, by the most positive arguments,[3] that all our past is self-preserved in us, that this preservation only makes one with the musical character of duration, with the indivisible nature of change, but that one part only is conscious of it, the part concerned with action, to which present conceptions supply a body of actuality.

What we call our present must be conceived neither as a mathematical point nor

[1] *Revue de Métaphysique et de Morale*, November 1904.

[2] An extremely suggestive résumé of these theses will be found in the second lecture on *The Perception of Change*.

[3] Instead of brutally connecting the two extremes of matter and mind, one regarded in its highest action, the other in its most rudimentary mechanism, thus dooming to certain failure any attempt to explain their actual union, Mr Bergson studies their living contact at the point of intersection marked by the phenomena of perception and memory: he compares the higher point of matter—the brain—and the lower point of mind—certain recollections —and it is between these two neighbouring points that he notes a difference, by a method no longer dialectic but experimental.

as a segment with precise limits: it is the moment of our history brought out by our attention to life, and nothing, in strict justice, would prevent it from extending to the whole of this history. It is not recollection then, but forgetfulness which demands explanation.

According to a dictum of Ravaisson, of which Mr Bergson makes use, the explanation must be sought in the body: "it is materiality which causes forgetfulness in us."

There are, in fact, several planes of memory, from "pure recollection" not yet interpreted in distinct images down to the same recollection actualised in embryo sensations and movements begun; and we descend from the one to the other, from the life of simple "dream" to the life of practical "drama," along "dynamic schemes." The last of these planes is the body; a simple instrument of action, a bundle of motive habits, a group of mechanisms which mind has set up to act. How does it operate in the work of memory? The task of the brain is every moment to thrust back into unconsciousness all that part of our past which is not at the time useful. Minute study of facts shows that the brain is employed in choosing from the past, in diminishing, simplifying, and extracting from it all that can contribute to present experience; but it is not concerned to preserve it. In short, the brain can only explain *absences*, not *presences*. That is why the analysis of memory illustrates the reality of mind, and its independence relative to matter. Thus is determined the relation of soul to body, the penetrating point which it inserts and drives into the plane of action. " Mind borrows from matter perceptions from which it derives its nourishment, and gives them back to it in the form of movement, on which it has impressed its liberty."[1]

This, then, is how the cycle of research closes, by returning to the initial problem, the problem of perception. In the two opposing systems by which attempts have been made to solve it, Mr Bergson discovers a common postulate, resulting in a common impotence. From the idealistic point of view we do not succeed in explaining how a world is expressed externally, nor from the realistic point of view how an ego is expressed internally. And this double failure comes again from the underlying hypothesis, according to which the duality of the subject and object is conceived as primitive, radical, and static. Our duty is dia-

[1] *Matter and Memory*, p. 279.

THE PROBLEM OF CONSCIOUSNESS 199

metrically opposed. We have to consider this duality as gradually elaborated, and the problem concerning it must be first stated, and then solved as a function of time rather than of space. Our representation begins by being impersonal, and it is only later that it adopts our body as centre. We emerge gradually from universal reality, and our realising roots are always sunk in it. But this reality in itself is already consciousness, and the first moment of perception always puts us back into the initial state previous to the separation of the subject and object. It is by the work of life, and by action, that this separation is effected, created, accentuated, and fixed. And the common mistake of realism and idealism is to believe it effected in advance, whereas it is relatively second to perception.

Hence comes the absolute value of immediate intuition. For from what source could an irreducible relativity be produced in it? It would be absurd to make it depend on the constitution of our brain, since our brain itself, so far as it is a group of images, is only a part of the universe, presenting the same characteristics as the whole; and in so far as it is a group of mechanisms become habits, is only a result of the initial action of life, of original perceptive discernment. And, on the other hand, no less absurd would be the fear that the subject can ever be excluded or eliminated from its own knowledge, since, in reality, the subject, like the object, is in perception, not perception in the subject—at least not primitively. So that it is by a trick of speech that the theses of fundamental relativity take root: they vanish when we return to immediacy; that is to say, when we present problems as they ought to be presented, in terms which do not suppose any conceptual analysis yet accomplished.

VI
THE PROBLEM OF EVOLUTION: LIFE AND MATTER

AFTER the problem of consciousness Mr Bergson was bound to approach that of evolution, for psychological liberty is only truly conceivable if it begins in some measure with the first pulsation of corporal life. "Either sensation has no *raison d'être* or it is a beginning of liberty"; that is what the *Essay on the Immediate Data*[1] already told us.

It was easy then to foresee the necessity of a general theoretical frame in which our duration might take a position which would render it more intelligible by removing its appearance of singular exception.

Thus in 1901, I wrote[2] with regard to the new philosophy considered as a philosophy of becoming: " It has been prepared by contem-

[1] Page 25.
[2] *Revue de Métaphysique et de Morale*, May 1901.

porary evolution, which it investigates and perfects, sifting it from its ore of materialism, and turning it into genuine metaphysics. Is not this the philosophy suited to the century of history? Perhaps it indicates that a period has arrived in which mathematics, losing its *rôle* as the regulating science, is about to give place to biology." This is the programme carried out, in what an original manner we are well aware, by the doctrine of *Creative Evolution*.

When we examine ancient knowledge, one characteristic of it is at once visible. It studies little but certain privileged moments of changing reality, certain stable forms, certain states of equilibrium. Ancient geometry, for example, is almost always limited to the static consideration of figures already traced. Modern science is quite different. Has not the greatest progress which it has realised in the mathematical order really been the invention of infinitesimal analysis; that is to say, an effort to substitute the process for the resultant, to follow the moving generation of phenomena and magnitudes in its continuity, to place oneself along becoming at any moment whatsoever, or rather, by degrees at all successive moments? This fundamental

THE PROBLEM OF EVOLUTION 203

tendency, coupled with the development of biological research, was bound to incline it towards a doctrine of evolution; and hence the success of Spencer.

But time, which is everywhere in modern science the chief variable, is only a *time-length*, indefinitely and arbitrarily divisible. There is no genuine duration, nothing really tending to evolution in Spencer's evolution: no more than there is in the periodic working of a turbine or in the stationary tremble of a diapason. Is not this what is emphasised by the perpetual employment of mechanical images and vulgar engineering metaphors, the least fault of which is to suppose a homogeneous time, and a motionless theatre of change which is at bottom only space? " In such a doctrine we still talk of time, we pronounce the word, but we hardly think of the thing; for time is here robbed of all effect."[1]

Whence comes a latent materialism, ready to grasp the chance of self-expression. Whence the automatic return to the dream of universal arithmetic, which Laplace, Du Bois-Reymond, and Huxley have expressed with such precision.[2]

[1] *Creative Evolution*, p. 42.
[2] *Ibid.*, p. 41.

In order to escape such consequences we must, with Mr Bergson, reintroduce real duration, that is to say, creative duration into evolution, we must conceive life according to the mode exhibited with regard to change in general. And it is science itself which calls us to this task. What does science actually tell us when we let it speak instead of prescribing to it answers which conform to our preferences? Vitality, at every point of its becoming, is a tangent to physico-chemical mechanism. But physico-chemistry does not reveal its secret any more than the straight line produces the curve.

Consider the development of an embryo. It summarises the history of species; ontogenesis, we are told, reproduces phylogenesis. And what do we observe then?

Now that a long sequence of centuries is contracted for us into a short period, and that our view is thus capable of a synthesis which before was too difficult, we see appearing the rhythmic organisation, the musical character, which the slowness of the transitions at first prevented us from seeing. In each state of the embryo there is something besides an instantaneous structure, something besides a conservative play of actions and reactions;

there is a tendency, a direction, an effort, a creative activity. The stage traversed is less interesting than the traversing itself; this again is an act of generating impulse, rather than an effect of mechanical inertia. So must the case be, by analogy, with general evolution. We have there, as it were, a vision of biological duration in miniature; expansion and relaxation of its tension bring its homogeneity to notice, but at the same time, properly speaking, evolution disappears.

And further, Mr Bergson establishes by direct and positive arguments that life is genuine creation. A similar conclusion is presented as the envelope of his whole doctrine.

It is imposed first of all by immediate evidence, for we cannot deny that the history of life is revealed to us under the aspect of a progress and an ascent. And this impulse implies initiative and choice, constituting an effort which we are not authorised by the facts to pronounce fatalistic : " A simple glance at the fossil species shows us that life could have done without evolution, or could have evolved only within very restricted limits, had it chosen the far easier path open to it of becoming cramped in its primitive forms;

certain Foraminifera have not varied since the silurian period; the Lingulæ, looking unmoved upon the innumerable revolutions which have upheaved our planet, are to-day what they were in the most distant times of the palæozoic era."[1] Moreover, if, in us, life is indisputably creation and liberty, how would it not, to some extent, be so in universal nature? "Whatever be the inmost essence of what is and what is being made, we are of it:[2] a conclusion by analogy is therefore legitimate. But, above all, this conclusion is verified by its aptitude for solving problems of detail, and for taking account of observed facts; and in this respect I regret that I can only refer the reader to the whole body of admirable discussions and analyses drawn up by Mr Bergson with regard to "the plant and the animal," or "the development of animal life."[3]

As regards matter, two main laws stand out from the whole of our science, relative to its nature and its phenomena: a law of conservation and a law of degradation. On the one hand, we have mechanism, repetition, inertia,

[1] *Creative Evolution*, p. 111.
[2] *Revue de Métaphysique et de Morale*, November 1911.
[3] *Creative Evolution*, chap. ii.

constants, and invariants: the play of the material world, from the point of view of *quantity*, offers us the aspect of an immense transformation without gain or loss, a homogeneous transformation tending to maintain in itself an exact equivalence between the departure and arrival point. On the other hand, from the point of view of *quality*, we have something which is being used up, lowered, degraded, exhausted: energy expended, movement dissipated, constructions breaking up, weights falling, levels becoming equalised, and differences effaced. The travel of the material world appears then as a loss, a movement of fall and descent.

In addition, there is only a *tendency* to conservation, a tendency which is never realised except imperfectly; while, on the contrary, we notice that the failure of the vital impulse is most infallibly interpreted by the appearance of mechanism. Reality falling asleep or breaking up is the figure under which we finally observe matter: matter then is *secondary*.

Finally, according to Mr Bergson, matter is defined as a kind of descent; this descent as the interruption of an ascent; this ascent itself as growth; and thus a principle of creation is at the base of things.

208 A NEW PHILOSOPHY

Such a view seems obscure and disturbing to the mathematical understanding. It cannot accustom itself to the idea of a becoming which is more than a simple change of distribution, and more than a simple expression of latent wealth. When confronted with such an idea, it always harks back to its eternal question: How has something come out of nothing? The question is false; for the idea of nothing is only a pseudo-idea. Nothing is unthinkable, since to think nothing is necessarily to think or not to think something; and according to Mr Bergson's formula,[1] "the representation of void is always a full representation." When I say: "There is nothing," it is not that I perceive a "nothing." I never perceive except what is. But I have not perceived what I was seeking, what I was expecting, and I express my deception in the language of my desire. Or else I am speaking a language of construction, implying that I do not yet possess what I intend to make.

Let us abruptly forget these idols of practical action and language. The becoming of evolution will then appear to us in its true light, as phases of gradual maturation, rounded at

[1] *Cf.* the discussion on existence and non-existence in chap. iv. of *Creative Evolution*, pp. 298-322.

THE PROBLEM OF EVOLUTION 209

intervals by crises of creative discovery. Continuity and discontinuity will thus admit possibility of reconciliation, the one as an aspect of ascent towards the future, the other as an aspect of retrospection after the event. And we shall see that the same key will in addition disclose to us the theory of knowledge.

VII
THE PROBLEM OF KNOWLEDGE: ANALYSIS AND INTUITION

WE know what importance has been attached since Kant to the problem of reason: it would seem sometimes that all future philosophy is a return to it; that it is no longer called to speak of anything else. Besides, what we understand by reason, in the broad sense, is, in the human mind, the power of light, the essential operation of which is defined as an act of directing synthesis, unifying the experience and rendering it by that very fact intelligible. Every movement of thought shows this power in exercise. To bring it everywhere to the front would be the proper task of philosophy; at least it is in this manner that we understand it to-day. But from what point of view and by what method do we ordinarily construct this theory of knowledge?

The spontaneous works of mind, perception,

THE PROBLEM OF KNOWLEDGE 211

science, art, and morality are the departure-point of the inquiry and its initial matter. We do not ask ourselves *whether* but *how* they are possible, what they imply, and what they suppose; a regressive analysis attempts by critical reflection to discern in them their principles and requisites. The task, in short, is to reascend from production to producing activity, which we regard as sufficiently revealed by its natural products.

Philosophy, in consequence, is no longer anything but the science of problems already solved, the science which is confined to saying why knowledge is knowledge and action action, of such and such a kind, and such and such a quality. And in consequence also reason can no longer appear anything but an original datum postulated as a simple fact, as a complete system come down ready-made from heaven, at bottom a kind of non-temporal essence, definable without respect to duration, evolution, or history, of which all genesis and all progress are absurd. In vain do we persist in maintaining that it is originally an act; we always come round to the fact that the method followed compels us to consider this act only when once accomplished, and when once expressed in results. The inevitable consequence is that we imprison ourselves hopelessly in the affirmation of Kantian relativism.

Such a system can only be true as a partial and temporary truth: at the most, it is a moment of truth. "If we read the *Critique of Pure Reason* closely, we become aware that Kant has made the critique, not of reason in general, but of a reason fashioned to the habits and demands of Cartesian mechanism or Newtonian physics."[1] Moreover, he plainly studies only adult reason, its present state, a plane of thought, a sectional view of becoming. For Kant, men progress perhaps in reason, but reason itself has no duration: it is the fixed spot, the atmosphere of dead eternity in which every mental action is displayed. But this could not be the final and complete truth. Is it not a fact that human intelligence has been slowly constituted in the course of biological evolution? To know it, we have not so much to separate it statically from its works, as to replace it in its history.

Let us begin with life, since, in any case, whether we will or no, it is always in life and by life that we are.

Life is not a brute force, a blind mechanism,

[1] H. Bergson, *Report of French Philosophical Society*, meeting, 2nd May 1901.

THE PROBLEM OF KNOWLEDGE 213

from which one could never conceive that thought would spring. From its first pulsation, life is consciousness, spiritual activity, creative effort tending towards liberty; that is, discernment already luminous, although the quality is at first faint and diffused. In other terms, life is at bottom of the psychological nature of a tendency. But "the essence of a tendency is to develop in sheaf-form, creating, by the mere fact of its growth, diverging directions between which its impulse will be divided."[1]

Along these different paths the complementary potentialities are produced and intensified, separating in the very process, their original interpretation being possible only in the state of birth. One of them ends in what we call *intelligence*. This latter therefore has become gradually detached from a less intense but fuller luminous condition, of which it has retained only certain characteristics to accentuate them.

We see that we must conceive the word mind—or, if we prefer the word, thought—as extending beyond intelligence. Pure intelligence, or the faculty of critical reflection and conceptual analysis, represents only one

[1] *Creative Evolution*, p. 108.

form of thought in its entirety, a function, a determination or particular adaptation, the part organised in view of practical action, the part consolidated as language. What are its characteristics? It understands only what is discontinuous, inert, and fixed, that which has neither change nor duration; it bathes in an atmosphere of spatiality; it uses mathematics continually; it feels at home only among "things," and everything is reduced by it to solid atoms; it is naturally "materialist," owing to the very fact that it naturally grasps "forms" only. What do we mean by that except that its object of election is the mechanism of matter? But it supposes life; it only remains living itself by continual loans from a vaster and fuller activity from which it is sprung. And this return to complementary powers is what we call intuition.

From this point of view it becomes easy to escape Kantian relativity. We are confronted by an intelligence which is doubtless no longer a faculty universally competent, but which, on the contrary, possesses in its own domain a greater power of penetration. It is arranged for action. Now action would not be able to move in irreality. Intelligence, then, makes us acquainted, if not with all reality, at least with some of it, namely that part by which reality is a possible object of mechanical or synthetic action.

More profoundly, intuition falls into analysis as life into matter: they are two aspects of the same movement. That is why, "provided we only consider the general form of physics, we can say that it touches the absolute."[1]

In other terms, language and mechanism are regulated by each other. This explains at once the success of mathematical science in the order of matter, and its non-success in the order of life.

For, when confronted with life, intelligence fails. "Being a deposit of the evolutive movement along its path, how could it be applied throughout the evolutive movement itself? We might as well claim that the part equals the whole, that the effect can absorb its cause into itself, or that the pebble left on the shore outlines the form of the wave which brought it."[2]

Is not that as good as saying that life is unknowable? Must we conclude that it is impossible to understand it?

"We should be forced to do so, if life

[1] *Creative Evolution*, p. 216.
[2] Preface to *Creative Evolution*.

had employed all the psychic potentialities it contains in making pure understandings; that is to say, in preparing mathematicians. But the line of evolution which ends in man is not the only one. By other divergent ways other forms of consciousness have developed, which have not been able to free themselves from external constraint, nor regain the victory over themselves as intelligence has done, but which, none the less for that, also express something immanent and essential in the movement of evolution.

"By bringing them into connection with one another, and making them afterwards amalgamate with intelligence, should we not thus obtain a consciousness co-extensive with life, and capable, by turning sharply round upon the vital thrust which it feels behind it, of obtaining a complete, though doubtless vanishing vision?"[1] It is precisely in this that the act of philosophic intuition consists. "We shall be told that, even so, we do not get beyond our intelligence, since it is with our intelligence, and through our intelligence, that we observe all the other forms of consciousness. And we should be right in saying so, if we were pure intelligences, if there had not remained round

[1] *Creative Evolution*, Preface.

THE PROBLEM OF KNOWLEDGE 217

our conceptual and logical thought a vague nebula, made of the very substance at the expense of which the luminous nucleus, which we call intelligence, has been formed. In it reside certain complementary powers of the understanding, of which we have only a confused feeling when we remain shut up in ourselves, but which will become illumined and distinct when they perceive themselves at work, so to speak, in the evolution of nature. They will thus learn what effort they have to make to become more intense, and to expand in the actual direction of life."[1] Does that mean abandonment to instinct, and descent with it into infra-consciousness again? By no means. On the contrary, our task is to bring instinct to enrich intelligence, to become free and illumined in it; and this ascent towards super-consciousness is possible in the flash of an intuitive act, as it is sometimes possible for the eye to perceive, as a pale and fugitive gleam, beyond what we properly term light, the ultra-violet rays of the spectrum.

Can we say of such a doctrine that it seeks to go, or that it goes "against intelligence"? Nothing authorises such an accusation, for limitation of a sphere is not misappreciation of

[1] *Creative Evolution*, Preface.

every legitimate exercise. But intelligence is not the whole of thought, and its natural products do not completely exhaust or manifest our power of light.

Besides, that intelligence and reason are not things completed, for ever arrested in their inner structure, that they evolve and expand, is a fact: the place of discovery is precisely the residual fringe of which we were speaking above. In this respect, the history of thought would furnish examples in plenty. Intuitions at first obscure, and only anticipated, facts originally admitting no comparison, and as it were irrational, become instructive and luminous by the fruitful use made of them, and by the fertility which they manifest. In order to grasp the complex content of reality, the mind must do itself violence, must awaken its sleeping powers of revealing sympathy, must expand till it becomes adapted to what formerly shocked its habits so much as almost to seem contradictory to it. Such a task, moreover, is possible: we work out its differential every moment, and its complete whole appears in the sequence of centuries.

At bottom, the new theory of knowledge has nothing new in it except the demand that all the facts shall be taken into account:

THE PROBLEM OF KNOWLEDGE 219

it renews duration in the thinking mind, and places itself at the point of view of creative invention, not only at that of subsequent demonstration. Hence its conception of experience, which, for it, is not simple information, fitted into pre-existing frames, but elaboration of the frames themselves.

Hence the problem of reason changes its aspect. A great mistake has been made in thinking that Mr Bergson's doctrine misunderstands it: to deny it and to place it are two different things. In its inmost essence, reason is the demand for unity; that is why it is displayed as a faculty of synthesis, and why its essential act is presented as apperception of relation. It is unifying activity, not so much by a dialectic of harmonious construction as by a view of reciprocal implication. But all that, however shaded we suppose it, entails a previous analysis. Therefore if we place ourselves in a perspective of intuition, I mean, of complete perception, the demand for reason appears second only, without being deprived, however, of its true task: it is an echo and a recollection, an appeal and a promise of profound continuity, our original anticipation and our final hope, in the bosom of the elementary atomism which characterises the

220 A NEW PHILOSOPHY

transitory region of language; and reason thus marks the zone of contact between intelligence and instinct.

Is thought only possible under the law of number? Does reality only become an object of knowledge as a system of distinct but regulated factors and moments? Do ideas exist only by their mutual relations, which first of all oppose them and afterwards force intelligence to move endlessly from one term to another? If such were the case, reason would certainly be first, as alone making an intelligible continuity out of discontinuous perception and restoring total unity to each temporary part by a synthetic dialectic. But all this really has meaning only after analysis has taken place. The demand for rational unity constitutes in the bosom of atomism something like a murmur of deep underlying continuity: it expresses in the very language of atomism, atomism's basic irreality. There is no question of misunderstanding reason, but only of putting it in its proper place. In a perspective of complete intuition nothing would require to be unified. Reason would then be reabsorbed in perception. That is to say, its present task is to measure and correct in us the limits, gaps, and weaknesses of the perceptive faculty. In this respect not a man of us thinks of denying it its task. But we try with Mr Bergson to reduce this task to its true worth and genuine importance. For we are decidedly tired of hearing " Reason " invoked in solemn and moving tones, as if to write the venerable name with the largest of capital R's were a magic solution of all problems.

Mind, in fact, sets out from unity rather than arrives at it; and the order which it appears to discover subsequently in an experience which at first is manifold and incoherent is only a refraction of the original unity through the prism of a spontaneous analysis. Mr Bergson admirably points out[1] that there are two types of order, geometric and vital, the one a static hierarchy of relations, the other a musical continuity of moments. These two types are opposed, as space to duration and matter to mind; but the negation of one coincides with the position of the other. It is therefore impossible to abolish both at once. The idea of disorder does not correspond to any genuine reality. It is essentially relative, and arises only when we do not meet the type of order which we were

[1] *Creative Evolution*, pp. 240-244 and 252-257.

expecting; and then it expresses our deception in the language of our expectation, the absence of the expected order being equivalent, from the practical point of view, to the absence of all order. Regarded in itself, this notion is only a verbal entity, unduly taking form as the common basis of two antithetic types. How therefore do we come to speak of a "perceptible diversity" which mind has to regulate and unify? This is only true at most of the disjointed experience employed by common-sense. Reason, accepting this preliminary analysis, and proceeding to language, seeks to organise it according to the mathematical type. But it is the vital type which corresponds to absolute reality, at least when it is a question of the Whole; and only intuition has re-access to it, by soaring above synthetic dissociations.

VIII
CONCLUSION

As my last word and closing formula I come back to the *leitmotiv* of my whole study: *Mr Bergson's philosophy is a philosophy of duration.*

Let us regard it from this point of view, as contact with creative effort, if we wish to conceive aright the original notions which it proposes to us about liberty, life, and intuition.

Let us say once more that it appears as the enthronement of *positive metaphysics*: positive, that is to say, capable of continuous, regular, and collective progress, no longer forcibly divided into irreducible schools, "each of which retains its place, chooses its dice, and begins a never-ending match with the rest."[1]

[1] *Introduction to Metaphysics* in the *Revue de Métaphysique et de Morale*, January 1903. Psychology, according to Mr Bergson, studies the human mind in so far as it operates in a useful manner to a practical end; metaphysics repre-

Let us next say that until the present moment it constitutes the only doctrine which is truly a *metaphysic of experience*, since no other, at bottom, explains why thought, in its work of discovery and verification, remains in subjection to a law of probation by durable action. We have now only to show how it evades certain criticisms which have been levelled against its tendencies.

Some have wanted to see in it a kind of atheist monism. Mr Bergson has answered this point himself. What he rejects, and what he is right in rejecting, are the doctrines which confine themselves to personifying the unity of nature or the unity of knowledge in God as motionless first cause. God would really be nothing, since he would do nothing. But he adds: "The considerations put forward in my *Essay on the Immediate Data* result in an illustration of the fact of liberty; those of *Matter and Memory* lead us, I hope, to put our finger on mental reality; those of *Creative*

---

sent the effort of this same mind to free itself from the conditions of useful action, and regain possession of itself as pure creative energy. Now experience, the experience of the laboratory, allows us to measure with more and more accuracy the divergence between these two planes of life; hence the positive character of the new metaphysics.

CONCLUSION 225

Evolution present creation as a fact: from all this we derive a clear idea of a free and creating God, producing matter and life at once, whose creative effort is continued, in a vital direction, by the evolution of species and the construction of human personalities."[1] How can we help finding in these words, according to the actual expression of the author, the most categorical refutation "of monism and pantheism in general"?

Now, to go further and become more precise, Mr Bergson points out that we must "approach problems of quite a different kind, those of morality." About these new problems the author of *Creative Evolution* has as yet said nothing; and he will say nothing, so long as his method does not lead him, on this point, to results as positive, after their manner, as those of his other works, because he does not consider that mere subjective opinions are in place in philosophy. He therefore denies nothing; he is waiting and searching, always in the same spirit: what more could we ask of him?

One thing only is possible to-day: to discern in the doctrine already existing the points of a

[1] Letter to P. de Tonquédec, published in the *Studies* of 20th February 1912, and quoted here as found in the *Annals of Christian Philosophy*, March 1912.

226 A NEW PHILOSOPHY

moral and religious philosophy which present themselves in advance for ultimate insertion.

This is what we are permitted to attempt. But let us fully understand what is at issue. The question is only to know whether, as has been claimed, there is incompatibility between Mr Bergson's point of view and the religious or moral point of view; whether the premisses laid down block the road to all future development in the direction before us; or whether, on the contrary, such a development is invited by some parts at least of the previous work. The question is not to find in this work the necessary and sufficient bases, the already formed and visible lineaments of what will one day complete it. To imagine that the religious and moral problem is bound to be regarded by Mr Bergson as arising when it is too late for revision, as admitting proposition and solution only as functions of a previous theoretical philosophy beyond which we should not go; that in his eyes the solution of this problem will be *deduced* from principles already laid down without any call for the introduction of new facts or new points of view, without any need to begin from a new intuition; that his view precludes all considerations of strictly spiritual life, of inner and profound action, regarding things in relation to God and in an eternal perspective: such a view would be illegitimate and unreasonable, first of all, because Mr Bergson has said nothing of the kind, and secondly, because it is contrary to all his tendencies.

After the *Essay on the Immediate Data* critics proceeded to confine him in an irreducible static dualism; after *Matter and Memory* they condemned him as failing for ever to explain the juxtaposition of the two points of view, utility and truth: why should we require that after *Creative Evolution* he should be forbidden to think anything new, or distinguish, for example, different orders of life?

The problems must be approached one after the other, and, in the solution of each of them, it is proper to introduce only the necessary elements. But each result is only "temporarily final." Let us lose the strange habit of asking an author continually to do something other than he has done, or, in what he has done, to give us the whole of his thought.

Till now, Mr Bergson has always considered each new problem according to its specific and original nature, and, to solve it, he has always supplied a new effort of autonomous adaptation: why should it be otherwise for the future? I seek vainly for the decree forbidding him the right to study the problem of biological evolution in itself, and for the necessity which compels him to abide now by the premisses contained in his past work.[1]

The only point which we have to examine is this: will the moral and religious question compel Mr Bergson to break with the conclusions of his previous studies, and can we not, on the contrary, foresee points of general agreement?

In the depths of ourselves we find liberty; in the depths of universal being we find a demand for creation. Since evolution is creative, each of its moments works for the production of an indeducible and transcendent future. This future must not be regarded as a simple development of the present, a simple expression of germs already given. Consequently we have no authority for saying that there is for ever only one order of life, only one plane of action, only one rhythm of duration, only one perspective of existence. And if disconnections and abrupt leaps are

[1] For Mr Bergson, the religious sentiment, as the sentiment of obligation, contains a basis of "immediate datum" rendering it indissoluble and irreducible.

visible in the economy of the past—from matter to life, from the animal to man—we have no authority again for claiming that we cannot observe to-day something analogous in the very essence of human life, that the point of view of the flesh, and the point of view of the spirit, the point of view of reason, and the point of view of charity are a homogeneous extension of it. And apart from that, taking life in its first tendency, and in the general direction of its current, it is ascent, growth, upward effort, and a work of spiritualising and emancipating creation: by that we might define Good, for Good is a path rather than a thing.

But life may fail, halt, or travel downwards. "Life in general is mobility itself; the particular manifestations of life accept this mobility only with regret, and constantly fall behind. While it is always going forward, they would be glad to mark time. Evolution in general would take place as far as possible in a straight line; special evolution is a circular advance. Like dust-eddies raised by the passing wind, living bodies are self-pivoted and hung in the full breeze of life."[1] Each species, each individual, each function tends to take itself as its

[1] *Creative Evolution*, p. 139.

end; mechanism, habit, body, and letter, which are, strictly speaking, pure instruments, actually become principles of death. Thus it comes about that life is exhausted in efforts towards self-preservation, allows itself to be converted by matter into captive eddies, sometimes even abandons itself to the inertia of the weight which it ought to raise, and surrenders to the downward current which constitutes the essence of materiality: it is thus that Evil would be defined, as the direction of travel opposed to Good. Now, with man, thought, reflection, and clear consciousness appear. At the same time also properly moral qualifications appear: good becomes duty, evil becomes sin. At this precise moment, a new problem begins, demanding the soundings of a new intuition, yet connected at clear and visible points with previous problems.

This is the philosophy which some are pleased to say is closed by nature to all problems of a certain order, problems of reason or problems of morality. There is no doctrine, on the contrary, which is more open, and none which, in actual fact, lends itself better to further extension.

It is not my duty to state here what I believe can be extracted from it. Still less

CONCLUSION

is it my duty to try to foresee what Mr Bergson's conclusions will be. Let us confine ourselves to taking it in what it has expressly given us of itself. From this point of view, which is that of pure knowledge, I must again, as I conclude, emphasise its exceptional importance and its infinite reach. It is possible not to understand it. Such is frequently the case: thus it always has been in the past, each time that a truly new intuition has arisen among men; thus it will be until the inevitable day when disciples more respectful of the letter than the spirit will turn it, alas, into a new scholastic. What does it matter! The future is there; despite misconceptions, despite incomprehensions, there is henceforth the departure-point of all speculative philosophy; each day increases the number of minds which recognise it; and it is better not to dwell upon the proofs of several of those who are unable or unwilling to see it.

INDEX

Absolute, the, 113.
Adaptation, value of, 106.
Analysis, 18; conceptual, 43; contrasted with intuition, 52.
Appearances, 152.
Art, and philosophy, 57.
Atomism, 168.
Automatism, 98.
Automaton, of daily life, 86 *seqq*.

Being, as becoming, 88.
Brain, work of, 197.

Causality, psychological, 194.
Change, 182 *seqq*.
Common-sense, 15, 16, 18.
Concepts, analysis by and functions of, 39; as symbols, 44; creation of, 46; as general frames, 47; practical reach of, 50; inferior to intuition, 53; further discussed, 175 *seqq*.
Consciousness, 97, 165, 185 *seqq*.

Conservation, 85; law of, 206.
Constants, search for, 50; represented, 77.
Continuity, qualitative, 74.
Criticism, 36; of language, 38.

Deduction, impotence of, 117.
Degradation, law of, 206.
Determinism, 82, 192; physical, 85, 194.
Discontinuity, apparent, 78.
Disorder, 106.
Du Bois-Reymond, 203.
Duration, real, 80; perpetually new; 82, 87; and thought, 168; and time, 189; pure, 193.
Dynamic connection, 51; 174; schemes, 169.

Ego, encrustations of the, 71.
Eleatic dialectic, 177, 184.
Embryology, evidence of, 101, 204.

INDEX

Evil, a reality, 123.
Evolution, 85; drama of, 95; biological, 100; value and meaning of, 103, 201; not indispensable, 205; distinguished from development, 105; as dynamic continuity, 107; as activity, 109; further discussed, 121.
Existence, as change, 82.
Experience, 134.

Fact, 13.
Freedom, 83.
Free-will, 192.

Genesis, law of, 110.
Good, a reality, 123; a path, 229.

Habit, as obstacle, 107.
Heredity, 91.
Heterogeneity, 81.
Homogeneity, absence of, 74.
Huxley, 203.

Images, 27, 152.
Immediacy, 142, 154.
Immediate, the, 23, 24, 37, 150.
Inert, the, 132.
Instinct, 112; is sympathy, 116; contrasted with intelligence, 117.
Intellectualism, distrusted, 134.
Intelligence, 112; product of evolution, 115; and instinct, 118; broad meaning of, 120, 213.
Intuition, 20; as starting-point, 48, 53; intransmissible without language, 37; æsthetic, 56; triumph of, 58; and duration, 140; and analysis, 215.
Intuitional effort, 11; content, 19.

Kant, 62; his point of departure, 115; conclusions of, 157, 164, 212; escape from, 214.
Knowledge, absolute, 35, 36; utilitarian nature of, 45; new theory of, 218.

Language, 10, 167; dangers of, 173.
Laplace, 203.
Law, concept of, 104.
Liberty, 82; personal importance of, 84, 192 *seqq.*
Life, tendencies of, 90 *seqq.*; is finality, 108; is progress, 114; further discussed, 213, 215.
Limit-concepts, 180.

Materialism, 109.
Mechanism, psychological, 86; failure of, 94.
Memory, problem of, 8; perception complicated by, 33; importance of, 79; racial, 92; planes of, 197; memory of solids, 95.

Metaphor, justification of, 54–55, 75.
Method, philosophical, 52.
Mill, Stuart, 186.
Motor-schemes, 69; mechanisms, 72.
Mysticism, 113.

Non-morality, 120.
Nothingness, 106.
Number, 65.

Ontogenesis, 204.

Palæontology, evidence of, 101.
Parallelism, 66–67.
Paralogism, 196.
Perception, 25, 157; an art, 26; affected by memory, 27; further explained, 28; fulfilment of guesswork, 30; utilitarian signification, 30 *seqq.*; subjectivity of, 34; pure and ordinary, 158; further discussed, 162 *seqq.*; relation to matter, 165; perception of immediacy, 153.
Philosophy, duty of, 118, 119; function of, 144 *seqq.*
Phylogenesis, 204.
Planes, of consciousness, 65.
Progress, and reality, 72.

Quality, 33; and inner world, 77, 207.

Quantity, and quality, 79, 207.

Rationalism, 134.
Ravaisson, 137, 138, 197.
Realism, 136.
Reality, contact with, 11, 12, 16; a flux, 18, 33; recognition of, 33; absolute, 34; elusive nature of, 51; personal, 61; essentially qualitative, 73; pure, 76; inner, 86; contrasting views about, 93; further discussed, 179.
Reason, 219 *seqq.*
Relation, between mind and matter, 68.
Religion, its place in philosophy, 124, 225 *seqq.*
Renan, 128.
Romanticism, 121.

Schemes, dynamic, 169 *seqq.*, 180.
Science, 20, 21; prisoner of symbolism, 60; cult of, 128; impotence of, 131.
Sense, good, and common-sense, 149.
Space, 65.
Spencer, criticism of, 105; success and weakness of, 203.
Spiritualism, 109.
Symbolism, 175.
Sympathy, 36.

INDEX

Taine, 186.
Thought, methods of common, 49.
Time, required by Mr Bergson's philosophy, 22 ; in space, 80 ; and common-sense, 188 ; and duration, 189.
Torpor, 112.

Transformism, 101, 102 ; errors of, 105.

Utility, 17 ; as goal of perception, 160.

Variation, 105.

Zeno of Elea, 176.
Zone, of feeling, 78 *seqq*.

COSIMO CLASSICS

COSIMO is an innovative publisher of books and publications that inspire, inform and engage readers worldwide. Our titles are drawn from a range of subjects including health, business, philosophy, history, science and sacred texts. We specialize in using print-on-demand technology (POD), making it possible to publish books for both general and specialized audiences and to keep books in print indefinitely. With POD technology new titles can reach their audiences faster and more efficiently than with traditional publishing.

- **Permanent Availability:** Our books & publications never go out-of-print.

- **Global Availability:** Our books are always available online at popular retailers and can be ordered from your favorite local bookstore.

COSIMO CLASSICS brings to life unique, rare, out-of-print classics representing subjects as diverse as *Alternative Health, Business and Economics, Eastern Philosophy, Personal Growth, Mythology, Philosophy, Sacred Texts, Science, Spirituality* and much more!

COSIMO-on-DEMAND publishes your books, publications and reports. If you are an Author, part of an Organization, or a Benefactor with a publishing project and would like to bring books back into print, publish new books fast and effectively, would like your publications, books, training guides, and conference reports to be made available to your members and wider audiences around the world, we can assist you with your publishing needs.

Visit our website at www.cosimobooks.com to learn more about Cosimo, browse our catalog, take part in surveys or campaigns, and sign-up for our newsletter.

And if you wish please drop us a line at info@cosimobooks.com. We look forward to hearing from you.